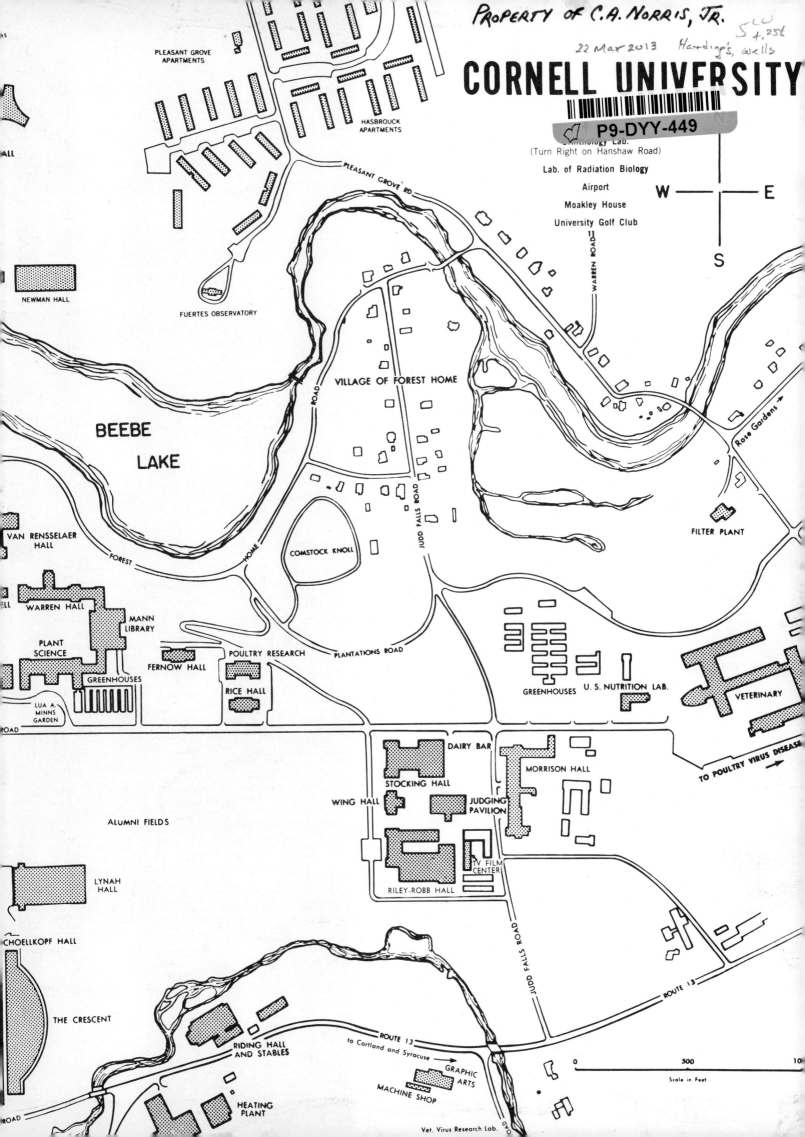

CORNELL IN PICTURES:
The First Century

"While breezes blow or waters flow
We'll honor thee, Cornell."

CORNELL IN PICTURES:
The First Century

Compiled by CHARLES V. P. YOUNG '99
New Edition by H. A. STEVENSON '19

QUILL AND DAGGER Alumni Association
Ithaca, N. Y.

For "Tar" Young '99, who made it possible,
this new edition of his book.

Library of Congress Catalog No. 65-17509

Copyright 1954, 1965 by Quill & Dagger Alumni Association

First published 1954   New edition 1965
First printing

Printed in the United States by Thomas J. Griffiths Sons, Inc.

Preface

Time has depleted the ranks of those familiar with the beginning and early development of Cornell University. Fortunately, many pictures of early scenes remain. Although pictures cannot present the many interesting incidents which attended the efforts of the Founders to give substance to their dreams of a great educational institution, they will, as they unfold the panorama of Cornell's architectural construction, framed in the beauties of a marvelous landscape, enable us to appreciate the intelligent foresight and the untiring perseverance of those courageous pioneers.

With thousands of pictures to be considered, limitations had to be set which have forced the omission of many important persons and events. Some of the pictures included, taken by themselves, may seem comparatively insignificant, but it is felt that with others and as contributions to a whole, they may help to convey the spirit of the institution and the aspirations of its Founders and of successive generations of teachers, administrators, and students.

It has been thought best not to attempt a strict chronological arrangement, because exact dating of many pictures would be difficult, but to assemble the contents roughly by decades. This will enable Cornellians to compare events of their own period with those occurring before and after, to see history as it were in the making, and perhaps to interpret more realistically the educational significance of the years spent in the "halls of learning" above Cayuga's waters.

Perhaps some may feel that undue space has been given to the physical environment: to the vistas of Lake and valley, to the beautiful walks, gorges, and waterfalls which charm every Campus visitor. Who can doubt, however, that a growing appreciation of beauty has enduring educational value and forms a part of the lovely and valued heritage conferred on every son and daughter by Alma Mater?

One who has seen the panorama of the past herein disclosed will ponder on its significance and direction and perhaps wonder what the future has in store. Ezra Cornell's democratic ambition—"I would found an institution where any person can find instruction in any study"—was indeed a noble one. The able and devoted Cornellians who for more than three generations have been carrying on his work may have come to feel that the fulfillment of his aspiration is impossible in a literal sense; perhaps they will now look forward to an institution where everything that is undertaken, to use words recently employed by President Malott, may be "well done and with distinction." Certainly great possibilities lie ahead.

Despite every effort to obtain accuracy, mistakes have undoubtedly occurred; the compiler and the publisher ask forgiveness and co-operation in making corrections.

Cornell in Pictures: 1868–1954 will, we hope, be expanded, supplemented, and improved on the occasion of the one-hundredth anniversary of this still-growing University.

C. V. P. YOUNG '99
Summer 1953

Preface to New Edition

As suggested by the original compiler, his book is now expanded to encompass the First Century of Cornell University. The excellence of the first Cornell in Pictures and thus its enthusiastic reception made this new edition possible. So this book is not only a record of the University's first hundred years; inevitably, like its predecessor, it must also be a memorial to "Tar" Young.

For many years as treasurer of Quill and Dagger Alumni Association he was its guiding spirit, and he conceived and painstakingly carried through the first Cornell in Pictures. He really sponsored it for Quill and Dagger: a triumph of his vision and perseverance. Brought forward from that book the reader will perceive Professor Young's abiding love for Cornell; his stubborn concern for the students here, especially their social and physical growth; his contagious joy in the natural beauties of the Ithaca region. These qualities endeared "Tar" to all who knew him. They are apparent in this book of his, I hope even as imperfectly amplified by his friend and admirer.

As Professor Young foresaw, corrections and additions have been made. His pictures are rearranged to fit a new format. The ten years from 1954 to the University's Centennial have been notably active and fruitful. Within limitations of space, selection, and this compiler's ability, this period is covered in the last thirty pages of pictures and text. The added index, it is hoped, will increase the book's usefulness and interest.

H. A. STEVENSON '19
November 1964

Acknowledgments

At its annual meeting in 1950 the Quill and Dagger Alumni Association adopted a resolution that money be appropriated over the next three years for the collection of pictures to be used ultimately in the publication of a pictorial history of Cornell University. Thus initiated and supported, the enterprise has been carried on and is now completed.

The task of collecting and selecting pictures and of identifying and arranging them in orderly sequence has been shared by many friends and Faculty associates. It is impossible to mention all by name or to assess the value of individual contributions, whether in pictures or advice. I am particularly grateful to Professor Emeritus F. C. Prescott (English), Professor M. G. Bishop '14 (Romance Literature), and Emerson Hinchliff '14 (Assistant Alumni Secretary), who as a "Committee of the Whole" have met whenever called upon, to pass upon selected pictures and suggested text, and whose aid has been invaluable.

Also, Mrs. Edith M. Fox '32, Curator and University Archivist, has placed at my disposal the facilities of the Mann Library Archives Depository, and my sister, Carrie V. P. Young '03, has patiently typed and retyped an endless series of corrections and additions entailed by successive developments. Many pictures have been contributed by the University Departments of Photo Science Service and Public Information. Other pictures were taken by Robinson Aerial Surveys, the 27th Division Aviation N.Y.N.G., John F. Brock '40, J. P. Troy, J. H. Fenner, and others. Several pictures are from the J. S. Barr '18 Collection and, of course, I have relied heavily upon the Cornell Alumni News.

To everybody, including the purchasers of the book, many thanks.—C.V.P.Y.

Addenda

Because of the success of Cornell in Pictures: 1868–1954 and to carry out "Tar" Young's wish that it be brought up to date to the University's Centennial, the Quill and Dagger Alumni Association at its 1963 June meeting authorized that this be done and agreed to finance publication of the new edition.

An advisory committee was set up to assist the compiler. Its members from Quill and Dagger were John Marcham '50, Walter W. Schlaepfer '51, and Herbert Snyder '16, president, treasurer, and secretary of the Alumni Association, Professor Morris Bishop '14, Emerson Hinchliff '14, W. Barlow Ware '47, and Paul L. Friedman '65, undergraduate president. From the University Mrs. Edith M. Fox '32, Archivist, and Robert A. Kidera, Assistant to the President and a co-chairman of the Centennial Celebration committee, also served. All were most helpful and especially, M. R. Kerns, University Printer.

To Professor Young's list of picture contributors this compiler adds his thanks also to C. Hadley Smith and Sol Goldberg '46. He thanks, too, both for new pictures and for information, Director of Athletics Robert J. Kane '34 and Director of Sports Publicity Benjamin E. Mintz '43, and the many others who noted corrections and additions to make this new book.

Special appreciation is due Mrs. Fox and all her staff of the University Archives and Regional History Collection for providing an ideal place to work and the best of interested assistance from them all in their beautiful Regional History Room in the John M. Olin Library. Without this help the new book would have been impossible.—H.A.S.

The Founder

Ezra Cornell (1807–1874) in his late fifties. This picture shows few traces of the years of toil and hardship through which he had struggled toward his goal.

Mrs. Ezra Cornell (1811–1894) in her early seventies.

"The Nook," the homestead below Ithaca Falls in which Mrs. Cornell brought up their ever-growing family while her husband worked as an itinerant salesman and later as a mechanic and promoter in developing what ultimately became Western Union Telegraph Co.

Ithaca Falls, with the wooden flume attached to the overhanging rock on the right side above it and the flour and plaster mills below. The mills were under Ezra Cornell's management from 1829–1839. (From a painting by Jefferson Beardsley, first University photographer.)

The Ithaca public library, Ezra Cornell's first considerable gift to his home town and one in which he took special pride. He was virtually its architect and builder. Begun in the spring of 1863, it was completed and conveyed to "the Trustees of the Cornell Library Association" in December 1866. Here the Cornell University Faculty held its first meeting, and in a basement room assigned to the DeWitt Guards and called Military Hall the first hurried examinations for entering students were given. Here also many student gatherings were held in later years.

The dam built by Cornell in 1838, long known as Beebe's Dam, created a reservoir of some twenty acres (Beebe Lake) and added to beauty of the natural waterfall (Triphammer Falls) in Fall Creek.

The 200-foot tunnel along Fall Creek that Ezra Cornell at age twenty-three blasted through solid rock to replace the wooden flume. It has been in continuous use since 1830.

The 1860's

At the formal outdoor opening of the University in 1868 George William Curtis, in the peroration of a glowing address, compared the new University to a newly launched ship: ". . . all its sails set, . . . its crew embarked, its passengers on board, and even while I speak . . . the ship begins to glide over the waves; it goes forth rejoicing, every stitch of canvas spread, all its colors flying." As he listened, says Andrew D. White in his Autobiography, "A feeling of 'goneness' came over me. . . . My mind was pervaded by our discouragements— . . . the demands of our thoughtless friends, the attacks of our fanatical enemies, the inadequacy of our resources. . . . Probably no ship was ever launched in a condition so unfit to brave the storms."

In later years in an address at an alumni dinner in New York City, President White portrayed the picture in all its stark reality: "The little body of teachers, the little library contained in one small room, the chemical laboratory contained in a small room in the cellar, the physical laboratory contained in a single dormitory room, the whole technical department contained in a temporary shed, the various colleges and departments which had no existence—lodging rooms without doors, lecture rooms inaccessible save by a cowpath on the Cornell farm, over streams and gorges without bridges, with a climb of 500 feet from the town to the single temple of learning [Morrill Hall] seated on a gravel-bank and surrounded by rail fences."

The "University on the Hill" pictured in 1868 from the cupola of the Clinton House. Dimly seen at top left is Morrill Hall, the one building completed. Near the right upper corner is Cascadilla Place. Just above the white "Cascadilla Mills" at left is the village burying ground through which ran the favorite short cut to the Campus.

Morrill Hall (also known as South Hall), the first building erected on the Campus, was named for Sen. Justin S. Morrill, author of the Land Grant College Act of 1862. It was barely completed at the opening in October 1868. It provided dormitory rooms at each end (for sixty students) and four lecture rooms. The small shedlike structure at the north end was the "power house" sheltering an engine which ran the hastily installed printing press. In front was a watering trough for horses. The center causeway led to the Shops; the one at right, to White Hall, which at the time of opening was half completed.

Cascadilla Place was planned as a water-cure or sanitarium, but when almost completed was acquired for the University. It proved a godsend as a dormitory for Faculty and students.

Southern entrance to the Campus from Cascadilla Place and the village. The first bridge over Cascadilla Creek was completed just the day before the University opened.

White Hall (North Hall), twin to Morrill and named for President Andrew D. White, who contributed generously toward its erection. It was the third building to be completed (1869) and, like Morrill (South Hall), provided dormitory and class rooms. It housed the College of Architecture on the third and fourth floors until 1959; now is occupied by the Department of Mathematics.

Northern entrance to the Campus. This foot-bridge near the site of the present powerhouse was the only bridge over Fall Creek between what is now Forest Home and the bridge below Ithaca Falls, now Lake Street. This was replaced from time to time by other foot-bridges, but vehicular transportation was not provided until Triphammer Bridge northeast of Sibley was built in 1898.

The Shops (long known as Old Chem Lab), the second building on the Campus, was partially ready at the opening of the University and later housed the Departments of Chemistry, Physics, and Electrical Engineering.

Andrew D. White was elected President of Cornell University in 1866, when he was thirty-four years old.

Founders and first Faculty of Cornell University. "Mr. White's career as president was not less remarkable for his choice of men of great learning and ability, and his persuading them to lecture at the University, than was his conception of a university and the vision of the one he had conceived."—Goldwin Smith.

1. Ezra Cornell, Founder. 2. Andrew D. White, President. Professors 3. Louis Agassiz. 4. C. Frederick Hartt. 5. Eli W. Blake. 6. James Law. 7. Lewis Spalding. 8. Maj. Joseph H. Whittlesey. 9. Burt G. Wilder. 10. William C. Cleveland. 11. Evan W. Evans. 12. Willard Fiske. 13. Theodore W. Dwight. 14. Goldwin Smith. 15. James Russell Lowell. 16. William C. Russell. 17. George W. Curtis. 18. William D. Wilson. 19. John L. Morris. 20. Ziba H. Potter. 21. Homer B. Sprague. 22. James M. Hart. 23. George C. Caldwell.

Morrill and White Halls completed, with rail fence still conspicuous. Space between was for McGraw Hall.

McGraw Hall (Middle Hall) was the gift of John McGraw, native Ithacan and one of the original Trustees of the University. It was to provide classrooms and house the Library and Museum, and its tower contained the chime and clock given by the McGraw family.

Cornerstone of McGraw Hall was "laid with all ceremony by the Grand Lodge of Masons of the State of New York" in June 1870.

John McGraw.

The Campus in 1871, showing the first five buildings completed, with fences and debris still cluttering the landscape.

The 1870's

This decade and the one following were to prove the most critical in the entire history of the University. An unexpectedly large enrollment of 412 students in the first year and an increase of about 200 in the next two years were followed by an almost continuous drop until in 1883 the attendance had fallen to 312. Not until 1884-85 did the number of students approach that of thirteen years before; but after this there was a marked increase. Among reasons offered for the decline were (a) failure of the University to realize the anticipation of self-supporting students; (b) increase of tuition from $10 to $25 a term; (c) higher requirements for admission; (d) adverse criticism from prominent educators and outraged ecclesiastics.

During this period of decline, and indeed in two later periods of great national depression, had not members of the University Board of Trustees and generous friends intervened to meet deficits and provide for immediate necessities, bankruptcy must have resulted. While no one could have rendered more loyal and devoted service than Vice-president William Channing Russell, the absence of President White upon several extended government missions accentuated the difficulties of the young University.

In spite of setbacks, however, physical growth continued and, upon President White's initiative, new courses and methods of instruction were adopted together with improved forms of organization and administration. The ship at last began to "glide over the waves."

Trustee Hiram Sibley.

Sibley Hall was the gift of Hiram Sibley of Rochester, an original Trustee of the University and first president of Western Union Telegraph Co. To this gift his son, Hiram W. Sibley, added shops for ironwork, woodworking, moulding, and the like. Under direction of Prof. John L. Morris a new system of manual training in mechanic arts later became an engineering curriculum of four years, leading to a degree in Mechanical Engineering.

Prof. John L. Morris.

Sage College was built and endowed by Henry W. Sage to carry out a stipulation of the Trustees "to provide for the education of women at the University a large college building, complete in all respects, with special recitation rooms, infirmary, gymnasium, dining room, and lodging rooms for 150 students." Opened the fall of 1874, "it lacked enough women students to keep ghosts out of dark corners."

Henry W. Sage.

The original University faced west, toward the valley. Chime and clock were in McGraw Hall tower.

Sage Chapel was the gift of Henry W. Sage, for many years a resident of Ithaca and for some twenty-five years after the death of Ezra Cornell chairman of the Board of Trustees. President White called Sage "the second great benefactor of this institution." Two conditions accompanied this gift: that the Chapel should never be delivered over to any sect; and that students should be attracted, but not driven, into it. The "chaplaincy" was endowed by Henry Sage's oldest son, Dean Sage, with the understanding that it was to be filled by leading divines of all denominations.

Sage Chapel interior, as originally built in 1874. Through the munificence of the Sage family the Chapel has been frequently altered and enlarged. The beauty of its decorations has delighted generations of students.

The "palatial" residence built in 1871-73 by President Andrew D. White at his own expense, where he lived until his death in 1918. The architect, William H. Miller '72, also designed the Library and Barnes, Stimson, Boardman, and Prudence Risley Halls. A south wing was added in 1911 and the President's House was remodelled in 1921 for President and Mrs. Livingston Farrand who lived there until his retirement in 1937. It was then occupied by President and Mrs. Edmund E. Day until 1951. In 1953 it became the Andrew D. White Museum of Art; the transformation assisted by a gift from Ernest I. White '93, nephew of President White.

Class of 1871: Where, oh where, are the co-eds?

Weather Signal Station, for many years a Campus landmark, indicated the forecast by displaying mammoth painted balls at the top of an eighty-foot mast.

Residence built by Ezra Cornell, incomplete at his death. It was first called "Villa Cornell," or sometimes "Cornell's Folly" because of its cost and also because of its location adjoining a cemetery. Cornell described the area as "a peaceful neighborhood." Some of the stone carvers and skilled carpenters brought from abroad stayed as residents of Ithaca. The house was occupied by members of the Cornell family for many years. Then it was purchased by Delta Phi fraternity and its name changed to Llenroc (Cornell in reverse).

From front of Sage College looking southwest: at right, the wooden bridge across a gully which "impeded progress" from Cascadilla Dormitory, particularly on rainy days. Beyond is the Arch of Victory for 1875 crews. The wooden building is the first Gymnasium, built with student and Faculty contributions.

The Campus from the steps of Sage College looking north: Sage Chapel in foreground, with Prof. Charles Babcock's house at right; in the background Morrill, McGraw, White, Sibley, and the Old Chem Lab.

Second view from cupola of Clinton House, ten years after the picture on page 9, showing changes in the village of Ithaca and "on the Hill."

Old barn of Ezra Cornell's farm, between the present sites of West Sibley and Lincoln Hall.

McGraw Hall

University Library.

University Museum.

The first Cornell crew to row at Saratoga, in 1873, was fourth of eleven colleges. Training at the time required a daily row of twelve miles, a long walking and running jaunt in the mid-day sun, thick flannels and sweaters to reduce weight, a restricted diet, and no liquid except one glass of water at breakfast, two at dinner, one at supper. No wonder that oarsmen were often afflicted with boils and unable to continue training. The 1873 crew: Stroke Charles C. King '75, Capt. Franklin Ferriss '73, Charles S. Dutton '73, James H. Southard '74, John N. Ostrom '75, Bow Rufus Anderson '73.

Boating at Cornell began almost with the opening of the University. The visit of an English educator and writer, Tom Hughes (author of Tom Brown at Oxford), developed great interest and clubs were formed. Crews sent to compete in the intercollegiate races at Saratoga in 1873 and 1874 made creditable showings. In 1875 and 1876 under tutelage of one of the crew members, John N. Ostrom '75, Cornell won both the varsity and freshman races; a leadership in college rowing that it held for many years.

The first sculling on Cayuga Inlet and the original boathouse which housed three variously rigged barges.

Class of 1875. Co-eds appear the first time in a Class picture. Facial expressions of their fellow-students merit study.

The three-mile, six-oared race at Saratoga July 14, 1875 (time 16 min. 53¼ sec.). John Ostrom '75, captain and coach, radically revised the stroke adopted and methods of training. He was rightfully given credit for the results achieved in both 1875 and 1876. After the finish of this varsity race, Cornell supporters for the first time burst forth with the inspiring "Cornell! I yell, yell, yell, Cornell!"

1875 Varsity crew. *From left. Standing:* Capt. John N. Ostrom '75, Charles C. King '75, James L. Jarvis '78. *Seated:* Daniel O. Barto '77, John S. Waterman '77, Edmund L. Gardner '75 (sub.), Albert R. Gillis '74.

Arch of Victory which greeted victorious Cornell crews of 1875 on their return from Saratoga.

The Varsity crew of 1876 on Cayuga Inlet in front of the first boathouse: Stroke, Coach and Capt. John N. Ostrom '75, John Lewis '75, James L. Jarvis '78, Albert W. Smith '78, Daniel O. Barto '77, Bow John S. Waterman '77.

The 1880's

In response to urgent appeals of Trustees, Faculty, and students President White, who had gone to Germany as US Minister in 1879, resigned and returned to Ithaca in 1881. Was he justified in accepting various government appointments during those critical years? Certainly there had to be a limit to the sacrifices he was asked to make. Besides the physical hardships he endured before completion of his President's House, he had burdensome administrative duties, meetings to be attended, addresses to be made, criticisms and attacks to be met. Although he often said, "Of all occupations, I know of none more satisfactory than that of a university professor," as President he availed himself of opportunities to escape an interminable routine of administrative cares which at times became "almost hateful." President White retired in 1885, but continued to live on the Campus.

University Faculty members in 1882, in all their wisdom and with all their varied types of hirsute adornment. At the turn of the century sixteen members of this group were still active. *From left. Front:* James E. Oliver, George W. Jones, T. Frederick Crane, William E. Lucas '75, Charles Babcock, Waterman T. Hewett PhD '79, John B. Webb. *Second row:* Horatio S. White, William A. Anthony, Estevan A. Fuertes, Charles C. Shackford, President Andrew D. White, George C. Caldwell, William D. Wilson. *Third row:* Irving P. Church '73, Henry S. Williams, Herbert Tuttle, James B. Burbank, Moses Coit Tyler, John H. Comstock '73. *Back row:* Hiram Corson, William R. Perkins, Albert N. Prentiss, Simon H. Gage '77, Abram A. Breneman, Charles F. Osborne, Isaac Flagg, Charles L. Crandall '72, Charles A. Schaeffer, George S. Moler '75, William G. Hale. *Not present:* D. Willard Fiske, James Law, John L. Morris, Isaac P. Roberts, Frederick L. O. Roehrig, Burt G. Wilder.

President Andrew D. White in his library after his return from Germany in 1881. This is now the main exhibit room of the White Library in Uris Undergraduate Library.

Old Armory and Gymnasium, built in 1883.

Franklin Hall, built by the University in 1883, housed America's first department (or college) of electrical engineering. It now houses the College of Architecture Department of Fine Arts.

Memorial Antechapel was added to Sage Chapel in 1883 by the Trustees and estate of Jennie McGraw Fiske in memory of Ezra Cornell, John McGraw, and Jennie McGraw Fiske. In the crypt are the bodies of these three and of Mrs. Cornell, Andrew D. White and his first wife, Alonzo B. Cornell (eldest son of Ezra, Governor of New York) and his wife, Willard Fiske, first University Librarian, and others.

Agriculture Faculty: 1. James Law. 2. Henry Shaler Williams. 3. Albert N. Prentiss. 4. Isaac P. Roberts. 5. Liberty Hyde Bailey. 6. George C. Caldwell. 7. John H. Comstock '73.

Footbridge over Triphammer Falls & spiral stairs into gorge.

Second bridge across Cascadilla Creek replaced the outworn wooden structure.

Frosh winners of Class Rush in 1883. In the early '70's the University tried to abolish underclass rushes because of injuries to limbs and clothing; in the fall of 1873 a Sophomore was suspended for instigating a rush. On leaving town, "The Sophomore was conducted to the station with carriages, music, and farewell speeches in which members of both Classes participated." Rushes were soon resumed.

What is now Central Avenue had this wooden bridge across a gully just south of the present Campus Road. Students celebrating Hallowe'en October 31, 1882 wreaked havoc with the bridge (*right*). Penalty: one term suspension for ten ringleaders and $400 cost of repair.

Military drill on the Campus. Old Chem Lab is at left; Faculty homes along East Avenue; President's House at right. (*Right*) Cowpath above Ithaca cemetery, used as a highway from the village.

Sibley College, Shops, Mechanical Laboratory. Cornell was first to establish machine shops for its Engineering courses, and under Robert H. Thurston's direction Sibley College rapidly rose to be one of the largest and best engineering schools. He trained engineers who carried on his ideas all over the world. "Few days in the history of Cornell," President White said, "were so fraught with good as that on which Thurston accepted the call to head Sibley College."

Prof. "Bobby" Thurston at his Sibley class in Thermodynamics.

The Foundry, with Bob and Jim Vanderhoef and Sibley students.

The first Wood Shop.

Andrew D. White, retiring in 1885, nominated as his successor Charles Kendall Adams, professor of history at University of Michigan. His tenure of seven years was an era of important development. Almost every part of the University organization was affected: requirements for admission and for degrees were advanced, courses of study were simplified, better relations with secondary schools were established, and students increased threefold.

Other developments included a much-strengthened Classical Department, an Agricultural Experiment Station, a Department of Horticulture, and the Sage School of Philosophy. Many needed buildings were added: Lincoln, Barnes, Boardman Halls and an imposing Library ranking among the best in the country. Particularly should President Adams be remembered for notable appointments to the Faculty: Jacob Gould Schurman, Liberty Hyde Bailey, Francis M. Burdick, George L. Burr '81, Rolla C. Carpenter MME '88, William F. Durand, William A. Finch '80, Ernest W. Huffcut '84, Jeremiah W. Jenks, Edward L. Nichols '75, Harris J. Ryan '87, Ralph S. Tarr, Benjamin Ide Wheeler, Walter F. Willcox.

President Adams in President's Chair.

President White at retirement.

University Faculty on the steps of Morrill Hall. President Charles Kendall Adams stands against balustrade at right.

Second suspension bridge across Fall Creek. It was the main entrance to the Campus from the north.

(1880's) 23

The Campus from Sage College, with the Fiske-McGraw mansion in left background. The mansion was begun by Jennie McGraw shortly before a stay in Europe, where she and Willard Fiske were married in 1880. Returning because of failing health, she died the following year before the house was completed. Beautifully designed, decorated, and landscaped at a cost exceeding $300,000, it was unoccupied for many years. It was later occupied by Chi Psi fraternity until destroyed by fire in 1906.

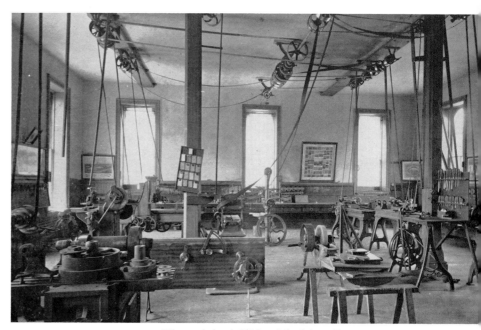

The original Sibley Machine Shop.

Sibley Blacksmith Shop, with William F. ("Old Man") Head, his nephew, and students.

Later Machine Shop.

Towers of Cornell.

University Barn, site of Comstock Hall, former Home Economics building.

Plug-hat group: Seniors '85.

Millstream running from Eddy's Dam to Eddy's Cotton Mill, formerly on the site of Cascadilla Hall.

Steps and bridge leading from millstream to Central Avenue and bridge across Cascadilla Gorge.

Students' recreation area in late '80's. *Right:* South half of Campus from McGraw Hall tower, showing Library started

(lower right) with Sage Chapel, Barnes Hall, and Sage College *(center)*, and Faculty homes on East & Central Avenues.

Prof. Burt G. Wilder and his Freshman class in the basement of McGraw Hall. Recommended to President White by Louis Agassiz, Prof. Wilder was one of the first three members of the Faculty to be approved by the Trustees. For many years his course of "extemporaneous" lectures on human physiology was required for all Freshmen.

The "entire" student body (perhaps 800 of some 1000 total) with many Faculty members (President Schurman center front in Norfolk jacket) pictured on the slope southeast of East Sibley site.

Class of 1887.

Barnes Hall. The Cornell University Christian Association was organized in 1869 by twelve students, two of whom entered the ministry. First meetings were in Cascadilla Place and then in various other buildings in town and on the Campus. In 1886 John R. Mott '88 became president of CUCA and initiated a drive for funds, raising about $10,000 from students and Faculty. Alfred S. Barnes added a gift of $45,000 and Barnes Hall was completed in 1888. It served as a religious center for sixty-three years, also providing an athletic trophy room, the Cornell Co-op (now Campus Store) moved from Morrill Hall basement, and various rooms for cultural purposes. Cornell United Religious Work (CURW) moved to the new Anabel Taylor Hall in 1952.

Stone bench placed under pine tree near the site of Stimson Hall in 1871 by Goldwin Smith bears inscription, "Above All Nations Is Humanity." Bench is now in front of Goldwin Smith Hall.

Baseball game on the Campus near the Old Chem Lab; Harry L. Taylor '88 catching: Columbia 6, Cornell 4.

The Campus from the north, showing a later baseball field on the Quadrangle.

Cornell's second intercollegiate track team, 1886. *From left. Front:* Theodore Hersey '88, John Wilkinson '89, G. F. Roess '90, F. L. Dodgson '89. *Middle:* George McCann '86, W. Z. Morrison '87, E. L. Smith '86, Frank McFarland '89. *Back:* J. S. Parker '89, H. E. Summers '87, C. W. Horr '87, P. B. Roberts '87 (pres. Athletic Assn.), F. V. Coville '87, A. C. Balch '89, F. T. Howard '86.

Cornell records at this time: 100 yds. 10⅖ sec. C. W. Horr '87; 220 yds. 23⅖ sec. Horr; 440 yds. 53⅕ sec. F. V. Coville '87; ½ mile 2 min. 11 ⅖ sec. H. E. Summers '87; mile 4 min. 55 sec. Summers; 10 hurdles 3 ft. 6 in. Coville; 120-yd. low hurdles 18⅕ sec. Coville; mile walk 8 min. 19 sec. J. H. Grotecloss '84; hammer throw 73 ft. 10 in. W. Z. Morrison '87; standing broad jump 9 ft. 10 ¾ in. W. B. Ruggles '83; standing high jump 4 ft. 7½ in. Coville; running high jump 5 ft. 3½ in. G. R. White '88; 2-mile bicycle 7 min. 8 sec. C. R. Scott '89; rope climb 17 ft. 6 in. 6⅗ sec. G. L. Teeple '89; throwing baseball 379 ft. 6½ in. R. H. Treman '78; foot ball place kick 177 ft. 6½ in. W. F. Hamp '85; high kick 8 ft. 9½ in. Coville.

Lincoln Hall and behind it, across East Avenue, the house occupied by Presidents Charles Kendall Adams and Jacob Gould Schurman. In foreground is one of the arc lights which dotted the Campus. William A. Anthony, professor of Physics 1872-87, and his assistant, George S. Moler '75, later professor, developed the first successful dynamo in this country. The Cornell Campus was the first place in America, if not the world, to have a permanent installation of outdoor electric arc lights. *Right:* Arc light at Central Avenue entrance; Cascadilla Bridge replacing original wooden one.

Football on the slope east of Prof. Babcock's house (Sage College in background). This first intercollegiate game of "modern" football was with Union in preparation for a game with Lehigh in Elmira Thanksgiving Day 1887. Cornell lost to Lehigh, 38–10, in what was considered "a glorious defeat" because of a Cornell player's long run for a touchdown.

First eight-oared Varsity crew, 1889. *From left. Front:* Bow J. Dolph Ross '90, Stroke Walter S. Dole '92, Coxswain Louis W. Emerick '91. *Middle:* Aaron J. Colnon '92, William B. Tobey '89, Coach Charles E. Courtney, Capt. Guy H. Thayer '90, Herschel A. Benedict '91. *Back:* Herbert L. Barker '90 (sub.), Amos W. Marston '92, Percy Hagerman '90, Louis W. Healy '90. This and the next nine Varsity crews won every race except defeats in 1895 by Columbia at Poughkeepsie and by Trinity Hall at Henley, England, and in 1898 by Pennsylvania at Saratoga.

Wilgus Hall on State Street; now Rothschild's store.

University Faculty and buildings in 1889. *From left. Bottom row:* J. L. Morris, A. N. Prentiss, G. C. Caldwell, A. D. White, Ezra Cornell, C. K. Adams, W. D. Wilson, B. G. Wilder, J. Law. *Second row:* H. Corson, I. P. Roberts, C. Babcock, W. T. Hewett, E. A. Fuertes, R. H. Thurston, C. C. Shackford, J. E. Oliver, H. S. White, T. F. Crane. *Third row:* W. P VanNess, J H. Comstock, W. G. Hale, M. C. Tyler, J. G. Schurman, D. Boardman, H. S. Williams, S. G. Williams, B. I . Wheeler, E. L. Nichols, A. B. Canaga. *Fourth row:* L. H. Bailey, E. C. Cleaves, E. Hitchcock, Jr., C. A. Collin, E. B. Andrews, S. H. Gage, F. M. Burdick, H. Tuttle, H. B. Hutchins, G. W. Jones. *Fifth row:* B. G. Smith, C. L. Crandall, W. R. Dudley, I. P. Church, I. P. Roberts, G. S. Moler, S . B. Newbury, J. F. Kemp, H. C. Elmer, C. D. Marx, A. W. Smith. *Sixth row:* G. E. Fisher, C. A. Strong, C. Langdon, A. C. White, E. E. Hale Jr., J. O. Griffin, G. L. Burr, F. H. Hodder, J. McMahon, A. S. Hathaway. *Seventh row:* F. H. Noyes, W. A. Viall, L. M. Dennis, W. R. Orndorff, E. H. Preswick, O. L. Elliott, R. Anderson, H. A. MacNeil, B. W. Snow. *Eighth row:* R. F. Nelligan, E. W. Manning, H. K. Vedder, W. E. Simonds, W. L. Webb, H. S. Gutsell, F. J. Ryan, T. Henckels. *Top row:* W. H. Wood, H. D. Williams, J. M. Stedman, W. W. Rowlee, G. W. Harris, F. M. Bronson, V. F. Marsters, G. W. Bissell, G. Pollay.

The 1890's

In 1892 the Cornell world was startled by the resignation of President Charles Kendall Adams. Called shortly afterward to the presidency of University of Wisconsin, Adams continued as a successful administrator until he retired.

President Adams was succeeded at Cornell by Jacob Gould Schurman, Professor of Philosophy and Dean of the Sage School of Philosophy. Schurman was President for twenty-eight years, though he was absent two years, 1899 and 1912, on important government missions and his place was then filled by Professor T. F. Crane.

Many new buildings were erected during President Schurman's administration. Aside from those of the New York State College of Agriculture are the following: Infirmary 1895, Stimson Hall 1901, Sibley Dome 1902, Hydraulic Laboratory in Fall Creek gorge 1902, Carnegie Filtration Plant 1903, Goldwin Smith Hall 1904, Rockefeller Hall 1904, Rand Hall 1912, Bailey Hall 1912, Home Economics (now Comstock Hall) 1912, Prudence Risley dormitory for women 1913, Baker Dormitories for men 1914–1915.

During Schurman's twenty-eight years the number of students again increased threefold (1700 to 5500) and the Faculty grew proportionately. Cornell took her place among the more important educational institutions of the country. Largely through President Schurman's efforts the State College of Agriculture was established at Cornell and the Cornell Medical College in New York City. His administration was also marked throughout by an intelligent and consistent recognition of the relative responsibility of Trustees and Faculty in the government of the University, and by the encouragement of academic freedom.

President Jacob Gould Schurman in University's Inaugural Chair.

View from West Hill showing newly-built Boathouse on Cayuga Inlet, given by the Class of '90, and the University dominating the hilltop.

Cornell Cadet Corps drill on the Campus. At right Boardman Hall and Prof. Charles Babcock house; University Observatory in center background.

Cornell-Bowdoin crew race, the first college boat race on Cayuga Lake.

Skate-sailing on Cayuga Lake, 1891.

Student rooms.

Forest Home about 1890. Formerly Free Hollow, the community now has many Faculty residents. Note the highway bridge across Fall Creek and beside it old Bool Furniture Co. mill, last of numerous mills there.

Percy Field, downtown seven-acre playground, was presented by William H. Sage and named for Percy Hagerman '90, son of J. J. Hagerman who gave money to lay out and equip it.

1891 football team. *From left. Front:* W. D. Osgood '92, G. M. Bacon '93. *Row 2:* H. Floy '92, R. H. White '93, Capt. C. M. Johanson '92, E. G. Horton '92, C. J. Barr '93. *Row 3:* G. R. Harvey '93, G. P. Witherbee '93, B. Hanson '93, G. F. Wagner '93, E. A. Griffith '93, E. P. Young '94. *Back:* H. B. Strait '93, E. A. Moseley '95, L. H. Galbreath '92, A. J. Colnon '92, G. R. Baker '95.

Winter view southwestward from Sage College tower.

A Dairy group, Faculty and students. Standing at left are Profs. L. H. Bailey, W. W. Rowlee '88, H. H. Wing '81; seated, Profs. P. A. Fish '89, I. P. Roberts, G. C. Caldwell.

Original Dairy Building, now the north wing of Goldwin Smith Hall. At the end of road in center background is the University Barn, north of present site of Roberts Hall.

Testing Laboratory in old Dairy Building.

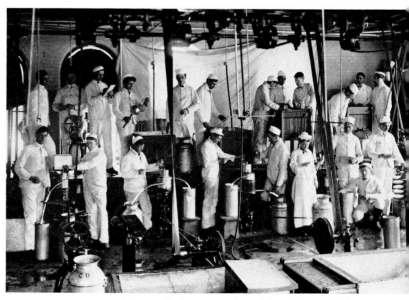

Butter Laboratory in old Dairy Building.

Old Armory decorated for Junior Prom in 1891. The first Junior Prom was in 1882 in Wilgus Hall, then the only opera house in Ithaca. The next year it was in the Ithaca Hotel; in 1884 and for many succeeding years, in the Armory. In 1887, it was related, the roof girders were completely concealed and thirty feet at the east end of the floor were curtained off for refreshments. The orchestra gave a concert from 8:30 to 9:30 preceding the dance, which lasted until 7 a.m.

The year 1890 marked the first appearance of boxes, as well as the employment of two sets of musicians, one for waltzes and the other for two-step, polka, and caprice. The Sophomore Cotillion was added in 1892, when the Junior Week program consisted of Masque, Tuesday; Cotillion, Wednesday; Musical Clubs Concert (Glee, Banjo and Mandolin Clubs), Thursday; Junior Promenade, Friday. In 1906 it was changed from a five-day period of much festivity with little work (the University being nominally in session) to a three-day period of greater festivity and no work at all.

Gymnasium Annex to Old Armory.

Gymnasium apparatus and gun racks on Old Armory drill floor.

Sage College and Green.

Morse Hall, Chemistry building, burned in 1916.

New University Library (now Uris Library) and Clock Tower (now McGraw Tower).

The President White Historical Library in the north wing; his own collection.

Corner of Central and South Avenues. At left is the Sigma Phi house. Home of Prof. Edward L. Nichols '75 is at right.

Demure co-eds of the 90's.

Senior Class '94.

Civil Engineering surveying camp group. Faculty members (*center*) include Profs. Henry S. Jacoby, Charles L. Crandall '72, Estevan A. Fuertes, Henry N. Ogden '89.

Women's eight-oared crew coached on the Inlet by Charles E. Courtney (*in chair*) and Frederick D. Colson '97 (*standing, left*), captain and coxswain of the Varsity crew. At Colson's left is Nan Gilbert Seymour '97 in male attire, and in middle of second row is Emily Dunning (Barringer) '97, both of whom became famous physicians. The Women's Boating Club was founded in 1897.

Student send-off of Varsity crew to Henley, England, 1895.

Junior Prom in the Old Armory.

Scrub baseball across Central Avenue from Old Armory (future site of Myron Taylor and Anabel Taylor Halls).

Junior Prom supper in Gymnasium Annex.

Library slope and Cayuga Lake, northwest from Sage College tower.

Campus and hills, southeast from Clock Tower.

Prof. Isaac P. Roberts with students in Agriculture.

Prof. Liberty Hyde Bailey (*standing right*) and a group of Horticulture students.

The one o'clock "Campus Centipede" on Central Avenue. At left, Sage Cottage built by Prof. Albert N. Prentiss, later the University Club.

Eddy Street Gate, "Andy's Chocolate Cake," given by Ex-President White.

Faculty baseball team 1895. *From left. Front:* ———, Charles J. Sembower, Adam C. Gill, Blin S. Cushman '92, Joseph Allen, Howard Cobb '95. *Back:* Henry H. Lannigan, William A. Hammond, Andrew C. White PhD '85, Louis M. Dennis, Wilder D. Bancroft, ———.

James Law Hall, Veterinary College, from tower of Sage College, with University Barn and site of Agriculture buildings in background.

Veterinary Faculty. *From left. Seated:* Veranus A. Moore '87, James Law, Simon H. Gage '77. *Standing:* Walter L. Williams, Pierre A. Fish '89, Grant S. Hopkins '89.

Prof. Grant S. Hopkins '89 (*back, right*) with his class in Veterinary Anatomy.

Prof. James Law, the "Scotch horse-doctor" brought from Europe in 1868, "rendered invaluable services to the State and Nation by eradication of common diseases of farm animals."

Zoology lecture room.

Prof. Willard W. Rowlee '88 (*in coat*) with Botany class.

Third Central Avenue bridge over Cascadilla.

University Infirmary, now called Sage Hospital. The first building, at right, was the home of Henry W. Sage, given to the University in 1897 by his sons, Dean and William H. Sage, with an endowment of $100,000. The Schuyler home (not visible) was acquired in 1911 as a nurses' home and the large building at left, built in 1912, is the main hospital.

Prof. Ernest W. Huffcut '84 (afterward Dean and adviser to Governor Charles E. Hughes) with his Law School class.

Eight o'clock "pathfinders."

Central Avenue.

Freshman Class of 1898 assembled on the steps of Sage College.

Cayuga Heights from the Clock Tower; Sibley Dome under construction.

A co-ed crew breaks training.

Baseball at Percy Field in the Gay Nineties.

1897 Varsity crew on Cayuga Inlet. It won two four-mile races at Poughkeepsie: June 25 beating Yale, Harvard, Columbia; July 2, Columbia & Pennsylvania. Bow S. W. Wakeman '01, W. Bentley '98, C. S. Moore '98, A. C. King '99, M. M. Odell '97, Capt. E. O. Spillman '97, E. J. Savage '98, Stroke F. A. Briggs '98, Coxswain F. D. Colson '97.

Frederick A. Briggs '98 (at 135 lbs.) stroked three Varsity crews in successive years.

John F. Moakley, new track coach & athletic trainer (1899), and Dr. Charles P. Beaman, medical adviser.

End of trolley line, from Boardman Hall porch.

Site of first State College of Agriculture buildings and of athletic playgrounds;
Veterinary College James Law Hall in left foreground, Observatory at right.

The 1900's

The early 1900's were highlighted by two very important additions to the University. One was Goldwin Smith Hall (1904–06) for the College of Arts & Sciences, named for one of Cornell's most eminent professors. In his will Prof. Goldwin Smith left the University in 1910 about $680,000 "for the promotion especially of liberal studies." He added, "My desire is to show my attachment to the University in the foundation of which I had the honor of taking part; to pay respect to the memory of Ezra Cornell; and to show my attachment as an Englishman to the union of the two branches of our race on this continent."

Another great addition to the University was the establishment by the State Legislature in 1904 of the New York State College of Agriculture at Cornell. Under the inspiring leadership of Liberty Hyde Bailey, who succeeded the first Director, Prof. I. P. Roberts (1873–1903) in 1903, was assembled a Faculty of specialists in agricultural research and practice which has probably never been surpassed in the history of agricultural education.

Suitable location of the Agriculture buildings aroused discussion. President Schurman's suggestion was finally accepted, that they be located not in the original Quadrangle adjoining the already constructed Dairy Building, but in the farm fields to the east. Thus happily was created a new Agriculture Campus.

The first Hydraulic Laboratory at Triphammer Falls.

Baseball was still played on the Quadrangle in 1903.

Prof. Goldwin Smith, English History, came to the youngest American University from Oxford, oldest university in the English-speaking world. He spent four years in residence here, 1868–1872, then made annual visits from his home in Canada and came to lecture at various times. At Goldwin Smith Hall cornerstone laying in 1904 (*above and below*), Prof. Goldwin Smith stands under umbrella; at left, President Jacob Gould Schurman; foreground, Prof. Charles Mellen Tyler.

Ex-President Andrew D. White wields shovel breaking ground for Roberts Hall. *Right:* Dean Liberty Hyde Bailey holds plow drawn by students to start first State College of Agriculture buildings.

Grading of the new Alumni Athletic Field gets under way.

Grading of Alumni Field completed. At right, first buildings of State College of Agriculture.

Chi Psi house (Fiske-McGraw mansion) from Morse Hall shortly before its destruction by fire December 7, 1906. Alpha Delta Phi is at rear and Alpha Tau Omega, at left.

Here the pictorial history becomes for a moment autobiographical. In 1903 the compiler was diverted from his ministerial aspirations by a three-year appointment as acting professor of Physical Education. At the end of one year the appointment was made permanent and the new professor undertook, with the approval and cooperation of President Jacob Gould Schurman and the Faculty, to build up a Department which, among other objectives, aimed to provide opportunity and incentive to the entire student body to engage in physical activity conducive to health and happiness.

The Cornell Athletic Association was an incorporated body independent of President and Faculty except in matters of student eligibility and leaves of absence. Only two full-time coaches were employed, Charles E. Courtney (1883–1920) and John F. Moakley (1899–1949). During this and the following decade, the rapid development of many and varied forms of intercollegiate athletic competition made necessary closer Faculty control.

President Schurman saw clearly the need of adequate facilities for outdoor sports. As a result of his initiative and persistence, a formal agreement was drawn up between the Board of Trustees and the Associate Alumni. By unanimous vote June 17, 1903, the Trustees accepted the proposition submitted by the Associate Alumni that "if the Board would set aside a suitable area of University lands, not alone for the athletic fields for intercollegiate contests, but sufficient to enable all undergraduates in the great future of the University to meet upon the democratic level of a student commons, the alumni would provide the means to build the commons for the outdoor sports of all Cornell students for all time." The Trustees designated about sixty acres of land east of Garden Avenue as "Alumni Field" for these purposes and alumni gave more than $300,000 for its preparation, more than meeting the terms of the contract.

John F. Moakley, football trainer and track coach; Charles V. P. ("Tar") Young '99, newly appointed Professor of Physical Education; and Hugh Jennings '04, baseball coach and all-time "great" in professional baseball.

Upper Cascadilla Gorge filled in for women's athletic field; now resurfaced for tennis courts.

Campus stone quarry, corner of University and West Avenues, supplied stone for the original buildings and many to follow.

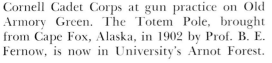

Cornell Cadet Corps at gun practice on Old Armory Green. The Totem Pole, brought from Cape Fox, Alaska, in 1902 by Prof. B. E. Fernow, is now in University's Arnot Forest.

'05 Senior Class of Law School; Dean Huffcutt at upper center and just below, Profs. Woodruff, Irvine, Pound, W. A. Finch.

Law School Faculty. *Front:* Cuthbert W. Pound '87, Francis M. Finch, Ernest W. Huffcutt '84, William A. Finch '80. *Back:* Edwin H. Woodruff '82, Frank Irvine '80.

The 1903 intercollegiate cross-country champions who finished first, second, fourth, and fifth at Traver's Island: Cornell 12, Harvard 37, Yale 46, Princeton 70; distance 6 miles; time 33 min. 15 sec., a record for the course. *From left (numbers show order of finish). Seated:* E. T. Newman '05, R. S. Trott '04, B. Smith '04, (2) K. W. Woodward '03, (4) T. M. Foster '04, (1) Capt. W. E. Schutt '05, (5) C. F. Magoffin '07. *Standing:* Manager S. H. Ehrich '05, H. F. Plumer '05, D. C. Munson '06, Trainer John F. Moakley.

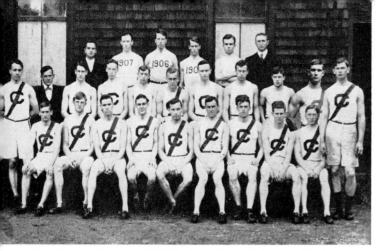

Varsity track team of 1905; first Cornell Intercollegiates victors. "Cornell won the meet by the work of a well-balanced team, not through two or three individual stars." *From left. Seated:* A. L. Willgoose '08, H. F. Porter '05, J. B. Philips '06, D. C. Munson '06, Capt. A. Vonnegut '05, C. F. Magoffin '07, F. W. Poate '05, J. C. Carpenter '07, T. M. Jackson '08. *Row 2:* J. N. Pew '08, Asst. Mgr. L. Woodland '06, H. M. Rogers '07, A. D. Camp '05, R. C. Turner '06, F. B. Townsend '08, L. Ashburner '06, J. C. Hemingway '06, G. W. Mosher '07, G. T. Cook '08, F. J. Porter '05. *Back row:* Mgr. S. H. Ehrich '05, L. M. Macpherson '07, H. S. Rowland '06, B. J. Lemon '08, C. A. Gould '07, Trainer J. F. Moakley.

Varsity crew of 1905, winner of the Poughkeepsie race (six contestants) by one-fourth mile. "Many experts agreed that it was the fastest crew that ever sat in an American shell." Coxswain W. G. Taylor '07, Stroke E. T. Foote '06, W. F. Lee '06, B. E. Fernow Jr. '06, G. W. Foote '05, J. P. Dods '08, Capt. C. E. **Boesch** '05, R. C. Barton '06, Bow W. S. Stowell '07.

Junior Week Carnival on Beebe Lake.

First Spring Day on the Quadrangle, 1902; Sibley Dome almost completed; Lincoln Hall & Dairy Building at right.

Right: President Jacob Gould Schurman and Ex-President Andrew D. White lead a Commencement procession.

Coach Charles E. Courtney and John Hoyle, later acting coach.

Observation train for crew races at Ithaca.

Toboggan slide at Beebe Lake.

President Schurman with his own toboggan.

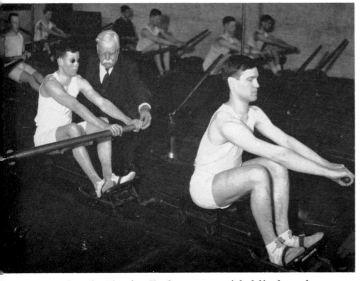

Coach Charles E. Courtney with blind students.

A blind student at stroke in practice.

Spring Day 1905: the bull-fight that rocked the nation. The Philadelphia Press published an outrageous story about the affair, and what was really a harmless and amusing burlesque, with an improvised "bull," brought upon the University unfavorable comment from all parts of the country. Typical: "The bulls came off the farm of Cornell University College of Agriculture, and had been specially overfed for the last week to make them good-natured." *Below:* "Matadors" and "picadors" were Mexican and South American students in authentic costumes; with the "bull."

Finish of Dryden Road Race, 11 miles, 1 hour 3 min. 8 sec. 1. C. F. Magoffin '07. 2. B. J. Lemon '08. 3. J. V. Colpitts '09.

Capt. Frank A. Barton, US Army, Commandant, and Cadet Corps officers.

Percy Field bleachers; guess who's winning, Cornell vs. Princeton!

1906 Varsity football team prepares for Thanksgiving Day game: Cornell 0, Pennsylvania 0. *Line:* R. Van Orman '08, C. C. Brinton '08, B. J. O'Rourke '09, W. S. Newman '07, E. I. Thompson '07, Capt. G. T. Cook '08, L. Babcock '09. *Backs:* E. T. Gibson '08, J. H. Jamieson '09, G. H. Walder '09, E. Earle Jr. '08.

Main reading room of the University Library.

Baseball at Percy Field; "Deadhead Hill" above the fence.

Winter on Beebe Lake.

President Jacob Gould Schurman *(right)* and Prof. Edward L. Nichols '75 *(left)* with Lord Kelvin, world-famous physicist and mathematician called "the Napoleon of science and the Columbus of submarine navigation and telegraphy," from University of Glasgow.

Sibley Auditorium, for long largest auditorium in University.

New Chime installed. Nine bells were given to the University by Jennie McGraw in 1868, to which one was added by Mrs. Andrew D. White in 1869 (the great tenor bell striking the hours). The original bells hung in a temporary wooden tower. From 1875–91 they hung with a clock in McGraw Hall tower; then were moved to the new Clock Tower of the University Library (now McGraw Tower at Uris Library). In 1908 four bells were added and in 1938 two more were presented by Charles K. Bassett '14, one in the name of his Class, the other in the name of his fraternity, Delta Upsilon.

Former President Andrew D. White addressing alumni on the fortieth anniversary of the University.

Goldwin Smith Hall Museum of Casts, imported by Henry W. Sage. Masterpieces of classical art, all but one are reproductions in full size, cast in molds formed over originals; most selected by Prof. Alfred Emerson, Classical Archeology.

Registration line at Morrill Hall.

Trophy Room in Barnes Hall.

Cornell Masque in "Oolong."

First class in Dairy Building east of Roberts Hall.

The first State College of Agriculture buildings, with Alumni Field rough-graded. Veterinary College is at left; Observatory, at right.

Goldwin Smith Hall portico by moonlight.

Spring Day

Underclass rush on Old Armory Green.

Freshmen captured in underclass rush and decorated for the Spring Day parade.

"Peerade": A preview of things to come.

Architects blow their own horns.

Law and order must prevail!

Raucous sideshow barkers.

Pocohontas saves John Smith's life!

Teddy Roosevelt the Hunter!

Fun, thrills, glamour, at grand and glorious Spring Day Circus!

Crowd on Sage College Green.

Prof. C. A. Martin '90 with class in the Architecture drafting room, top floor of White Hall.

Start of annual intramural cross-country race, Sage Green.

Underclass pushball contest between halves of a football game on Percy Field.

Intercollege baseball game on Alumni Field.

College of Architecture Christmas party.

Fall Creek and first University Powerhouse.

Cornell Cadet Corps Band.

Goldwin Smith Walk along Cascadilla Creek.

Forest Home Walk along Beebe Lake.

Cadet Corps dress parade on the Quadrangle.

Stewart Avenue bridge over Fall Creek.

Cascadilla Dormitory.

Goldwin Smith Hall completed.

Tenth annual convention, Association of American Universities, at Cornell 1909. *From left. Front:* Presidents Hill (Missouri), Schurman (Cornell), Northrop (Minnesota), Angell (Michigan), Eliot (Harvard), Prof. Baldwin (Johns Hopkins). Between Northrop & Angell is Prof. Monroe Smith, Columbia. *Back rows:* Profs. Ames (Pennsylvania), Magie (Princeton), Stratton (California), Fine (Princeton), Willcox (Cornell), Page (Virginia), Warren (Harvard), Carpenter (Columbia), Crothers (Stanford), Kinley (Illinois), Vaughn (Michigan), Bolling (Catholic University of America).

The Cosmopolitan Club, representing twenty-one nationalities in its charter membership, at its new home. The Club was founded in 1904 "primarily for the purpose of bringing the foreign students into a common fellowship, while serving also as an international clearing house of ideas."

Former President Andrew D. White approaches the Old Armory to hear Acting President T. F. Crane deliver address to open a new year, September 25, 1912.

President and dignitaries. *From left:* Jacob Gould Schurman, Charles M. Schwab, Trustees Mynderse Van Cleef '74 & George C. Boldt, Proctor T. H. Twesten, John C. Westervelt '94, Trustee J. DuPratt White '90.

The 1910's

Until the United States entered the World War in 1917, building continued over the entire Campus.

The rapid development of the University can be realized by a glance at the appropriations made in one year for buildings planned or partially completed: Prudence Risley Hall for women $300,000; Home Economics $154,000; Bailey Hall $138,000; Veterinary College buildings $140,000; Infirmary Addition $120,000; Poultry Building $90,000; Rand Hall $65,000; Heating Plant $50,000; New Barn $20,000. In addition, plans for a group of residential halls for men were prepared and with the enthusiastic initiative of Trustee George C. Boldt anonymous gifts were announced one after another for construction of the Baker Dormitories.

As has been said, the growth of the College of Agriculture was due in large measure to Dean L. H. Bailey's genius and far-reaching plans. It was with a general feeling of dismay, therefore, that his resignation was received in 1912. He desired "to devote himself to travel and study, and to carry out plans for the remainder of his life which he had formed many years ago."

During the same year President Jacob Gould Schurman took his first real vacation in many years and accepted for his "sabbatic" a year's appointment as US Minister to Greece. He left as Acting President for the second time Prof. T. F. Crane.

President's Avenue.

Cascadilla Gorge.

Class secretaries in 1910. *Front:* J. H. Comstock '73, V. A. Moore '87, A. F. Matthews '83, W. W. Rowlee '88, W. J. Norton '02, W. A. Finch '80, Edwin Gillette '74, Woodford Patterson '95. *Middle:* G. H. Young '00, C. J. Miller '90, L. Coville '86, C. H. Tuck '06, S. W. Shoemaker '08, R. J. Eidlitz '84. *Back:* D. J. Miller '10, C. S. Northup '93. H. J. Richardson '05, W. F. Atkinson '95, C. D. Bostwick '92.

Bailey Hall, University auditorium built by New York State and named for Liberty Hyde Bailey *(right)*.

Bacon Baseball Cage, named for George W. Bacon '92, who was chairman of the Associate Alumni committee that raised funds for Alumni Field.

Prudence Risley Hall, dormitory for women. Gift of Mrs. Russell Sage; named for her mother.

Andrew D. White in his eighties.

Former US President William H. Taft and President Schurman.

Stanton Griffis '10 reading his Senior Class History. He later represented the United States in many countries.

Dedication of the Andrew D. White Statue, 1915; Dean T. F. Crane speaking.

Baker Dormitories, the first for men, below West Avenue. Their Collegiate Gothic style was characterized by Ralph Adams Cram as "one of the few very perfect and supremely beautiful architectural styles."

Prof. Louis M. Dennis looks in on a Chemistry laboratory.

Machine Shop in Rand Hall.

Capacity attendance at a baseball and a football game on Percy Field.

Start of Intercollegiate cross-country race from Old Armory
Green, 1912; won by Harvard; J. P. Jones '13 (82), first.

The Intercollegiate track meet at Cambridge, Mass., May 27, 1911, considered the greatest thus far held, was a triumph for Coach John F. Moakley and his men. John Paul Jones '13 set a world record for the mile of 4 min. 15 ⅖ sec. and an Intercollegiates record in the half-mile of 1:54 ⅘. Tell Berna '12 set a two-mile Intercollegiates record of 9:25 ⅕. The same day, Cornell won a fourteen-inning baseball game from Yale at Ithaca and the Freshmen won from Dartmouth at Hanover. Cornell Varsity and Freshman crews beat Harvard at Ithaca and the Junior Varsity led Navy, Yale, Harvard, and Penn at Philadelphia. The Boston Transcript paid this glowing tribute: "Next to the honor of beating Cornell is the honor of being beaten by men who play the game like gentlemen, men who can generously win and as handsomely take a defeat."

Intercollegiate track champions 1911. *From left. Front:* H. N. Putnam '12, J. P. Jones '13, H. H. D'Autremont '11, H. W. Ford '11, Capt. E. G. MacArthur '11, V. A. Stibolt '11, H. G. Kanzler '13, T. S. Berna '12, S. F. Nixon '11. *Row 2:* Coach J. F. Moakley, S. H. Stevenson '12, E. A. MacKrell '11, E. A. Hunger '12, A. S. Elsenblast '12, J. W. Little '13, A. E. Bannister '13, C. E. Everingham '13, C. Crandall '12, Mgr. A. M. Roberts '11. *Row 3:* Trainer F. Sheehan, H. G. Curtis '13, J. E. Whinery '13, F. Ohrt '11, H. N. Hinckley '11, L. E. DeYoe '12, H. B. Liggett '12, H. H. Snyder '13, W. H. Bennett '13, H. Flack '12, P. D. Brown '13, J. R. VanKleek '12, Asst. Mgr. W. W. Slaymaker '12. *Back:* W. L. Biggart '12, C. M. Gilchrist '13, L. S. Finch '13, W. D. Haselton '12, J. C. Hageman '12, A. H. Challiss '11, C. A. Major '12, C. W. Harper '12, J. L. Collins '12, D. W. Wallace '13, W. K. Wells '11.

Intercollegiate fencing champions the first time in ten years. Previous winners were always Army or Navy. Cornell 35, Army 34; the closest meet on record. *From left:* Capt. Dario Espindola '10, Philip W. Alison '11, Delmar G. Roos '11.

President Schurman at cornerstone laying of Schoellkopf Memorial Hall, given by Willard Straight '01 in memory of Henry Schoellkopf '02.

First football game at Schoellkopf Field, September 28, 1915, Cornell 13, Gettysburg 0.

The women's playground in Cascadilla ravine served admirably for pageants portraying legends and history, as well as episodes illustrating activities in which Cornell women had engaged. Nearly all the women in the University took part in the preparation and presentation of these events.

Coach Daniel A. Reed '98 (*left*) and Trainer John F. Moakley.

Coach Albert H. Sharpe at the head of his football stalwarts.

Four-mile relay world's record of 17 min. 43⅖ sec. was set in 1911 by *Middle row:* J. P. Jones '13 (4:21), L. S. Finch '13 (4:30), T. S. Berna '12 (4:24), H. N. Putnam '12 (4:29⅓). *Front:* J. L. Kraker '12, S. H. Stevenson '12. *Back:* Coach J. F. Moakley, C. A. Major '12, Mgr. A. M. Roberts '11.

Boathouse and Beebe Lake from the east. The Boathouse was destroyed by fire in 1918.

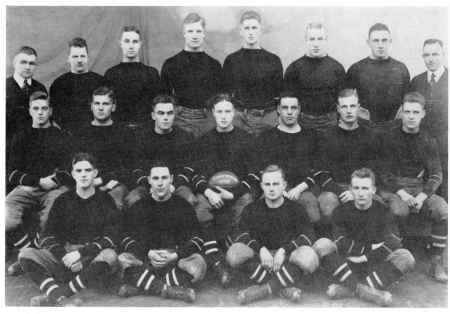

Undefeated 1915 Varsity football team; probably the best in Cornell's history. *From left. Front:* P. W. Eckley '17, A. P. Schock '16, F. P. Schlichter '16, R. J. Zander '17. *Middle:* F. T. Shiverick '18, E. E. Anderson '17, L. W. Mueller '17, Capt. Charles Barrett '16, W. C. Cool '16, M. N. Shelton '16, C. P. Collins '16. *Back:* Mgr. S. E. Hunkin '16, C. Tilley '17, C. W. Bailey '16, H. Snyder '16, R. W. Jewett '17, F. M. Gillies '18, P. P. Miller '18, Asst. Mgr. W. R. Lalley '17. Their record: Cornell 13, Gettysburg 0; Cornell 34, Oberlin 7; Cornell 46, Williams 6; Cornell 41, Bucknell 0; Cornell 10, Harvard 0; Cornell 45, Virginia 0; Cornell 34, Michigan 7; Cornell 40, Washington & Lee 21; Cornell 24, Penn 9.

The University Faculty, 1916.

1. M. W. Sampson	39. G. W. Herrick	77. C. E. Hayden	115. M. F. Barrus	153. H. E. Babcock
2. W. F. Willcox	40. Arthur Ranum	78. H. S. Gutsell	116. A. A. Allen	154. J. R. Schramm
3. S. H. Gage	41. C. T. Stagg	79. J. F. Putnam	117. R. W. Curtis	155. M. A. Lee
4. G. W. Harris	42. W. L. Williams	80. J. G. Pertsch	118. Laurence Pumpelly	156. E. E. Barker
5. I. P. Church	43. C. D. Albert	81. C. W. Hamm	119. H. D. Reed	157. R. P. Anderson
6. C. L. Crandall	44. W. B. Carver	82. F. O. Ellenwood	120. R. M. Ogden	158. E. W. Schoder
7. G. L. Burr	45. J. T. Parson	83. G. B. Upton	121. G. F. Warren	159. S. N. Spring
8. E. E. Haskell	46. J. McMahon	84. M. Dresbach	122. H. A. Hitchcock	160. P. H. Underwood
9. J. E. Creighton	47. A. P. Usher	85. H. W. Edgerton	123. R. S. Saby	161. M. Robinson
10. J. G. Schurman	48. C. E. Bennett	86. Cornelius Betten	124. Heinrich Ries	162. R. S. Hosmer
11. W. A. Hammond	49. H. N. Ogden	87. Paul Fenton	125. G. E. F. Lundell	163. E. A. White
12. Frank Thilly	50. F. A. Barnes	88. J. Q. Adams	126. E. O. Fippin	164. Virgil Snyder
13. E. H. Woodruff	51. A. C. Phelps	89. W. M. Sawdon	127. G. N. Lauman	165. W. E. Lunt
14. L. M. Dennis	52. C. S. Northup	90. G. R. Chamberlain	128. J. E. Rice	166. A. B. Faust
15. Nathaniel Schmidt	53. W. W. Warsaw	91. S. Stevens	129. H. C. Davidsen	167. P. R. Pope
16. Abram Kerr	54. A. E. Wells	92. C. M. S. Midjo	130. E. S. Guthrie	168. W. W. Comfort
17. E. L. Nichols	55. H. L. Jones	93. A. B. Recknagel	131. E. G. Davis	169. Royal Gilkey
18. G. P. Bristol	56. W. A. Hurwitz	94. J. K. Wilson	132. O. D. von Engeln	170. W. H. Rankin
19. D. S. Kimball	57. J. H. Tanner	95. H. A. Sill	133. Donald English	171. R. H. Wheeler
20. George Young, Jr.	58. E. N. Burrows	96. L. A. Maynard	134. Bristow Adams	172. E. M. Pickens
21. J. T. Quarles	59. K. B. Turner	97. S. Simpson	135. D. Lumsden	173. A. A. Peirce
22. H. S. Jacoby	60. G. W. Cavanaugh	98. O. L. McCaskill	136. P. A. Fish	174. A. H. Wright
23. H. H. Wing	61. E. M. Chamot	99. J. I. Hutchinson	137. E. W. Benjamin	175. V. B. Stewart
24. C. H. Hull	62. G. G. Bogert	100. G. S. Hopkins	138. M. A. Pond	176. R. A. Emerson
25. A. W. Smith	63. C. K. Burdick	101. Earl Sunderville	139. C. H. Berry	177. H. W. van Loon
26. V. A. Moore	64. S. S. Garrett	102. B. B. Robb	140. R. Matthews	178. C. E. Thompson
27. G. S. Moler	65. Miss Flora Rose	103. R. C. Carpenter	141. G. B. Muchmore	179. W. S. Foster
28. A. R. Mann	66. Miss A. Warner	104. A. J. Eames	142. J. A. Winans	180. H. J. Davenport
29. H. E. Dann	67. Miss B. E. Hazard	105. L. W. Sharp	143. C. P. Fitch	181. E. H. Wood
30. J. L. Stone	68. F. M. Blodgett	106. T. R. Briggs	144. Charles Gregory	182. S. G. George
31. Alexander Gray	69. A. P. Mills	107. A. A. Young	145. C. H. Myers	183. H. Hermannsson
32. A. C. White	70. J. B. Sumner	108. W. D. Bancroft	146. A. W. Boesche	184. W. M. Wilson
33. M. C. Burritt	71. Lane Cooper	109. G. C. Embody	147. J. F. Mason	185. E. G. Montgomery
34. W. N. Barnard	72. A. W. Browne	110. V. R. Gage	148. B. S. Monroe	186. J. A. Bissell
35. C. L. Durham	73. O. M. Leland	111. G. R. McDermott	149. J. G. Needham	187. L. D. Hayes
36. H. H. Love	74. A. C. Beal	112. Vladimir Karapetoff	150. A. C. King	188. L. N. Broughton
37. T. L. Lyon	75. D. C. Gillespie	113. John Bentley	151. H. A. Hopper	189. Lt. T. H. Tweston
38. F. W. Owens	76. D. J. Crosby	114. G. H. Collingwood	152. H. C. Troy	

Women's Class baseball teams line up before game hostilities begin.

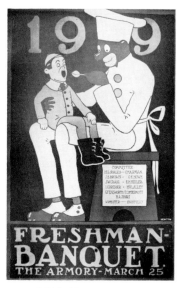

1919 Class poster.

Final baseball game for the interclass championship.

The broad jump.

Interclass field meet:

The high jump.

Archery on Old Armory Green.

Saturday hike through Buttermilk Gorge for Gym credit.

Girls' four-oared race on Beebe Lake.

Canoeing on Beebe Lake.

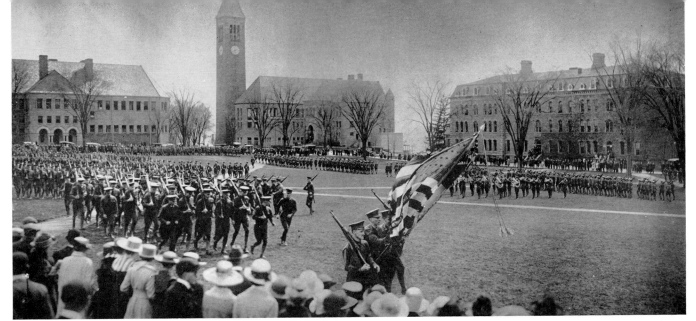

Inspection of the Cornell Cadet Corps (later ROTC) before US entered World War I. The University, as required by its Charter, has given instruction in military science & tactics since its founding. Until the practice was discontinued for ROTC units, Cornell was many times cited by the War Department after its annual inspections as a "distinguished college" in military training.

Cadet Corps pitches tents on the Quadrangle.

President Jacob Gould Schurman addresses enlisted students, World War I.

All intercollegiate athletics were cancelled when the US declared war April 7, 1917. Wearers of the "C" practice Manual of Arms on Old Armory lawn in front of Kappa Alpha house. *From front. Row 1 (right):* A. I. G. Valentine '17, J. M. Watt '18, P. P. Miller '18, W. D. Crim '17, W. Brown '17. *Row 2:* A. W. Richards '17, W. M. Dixon '18, P. W. Eckley '17, J. J. Quinn Jr. '17. *Row 3:* G. B. Howell '17, L. G. Brower '18, F. D. Boynton Jr. '17, I. C. Dresser '19. *Row 4:* F. T. Shiverick '18, A. L. Hoffman '18, A. W. Mellen Jr. '17, C. Burpee '17. *Row 5:* L. E. Wenz '18, F. K. Foss '17, L. V. Wingnagle '17, A. S. Harrison '17, T. C. McDermott '19.

Liberty Day celebration (June 1918) at Schoell-kopf Field.

Setting-up exercises in the Drill Hall—later Barton Hall (*right*).

Unveiling statue of Ezra Cornell June 22, 1919; Dean T. F. Crane speaking.

University Semi-centennial Celebration June, 1919. Dinner was served in Drill Hall to 4000 alumni.

Baker Court men's dormitories.

Entrance to Baker Tower.

President Jacob Gould Schurman's last Commencement address, June 1920.

Sage Chapel and the east Memorial Apse. In the Apse lie the remains of Mr. and Mrs. Henry W. Sage. Here the decorations were designed by artists associated in the firm name of J. & R. Lamb of New York City. The design represents a group of symbolic figures in mosaic or glass, representing education leading to the worship of God. The windows glow with pictures representing the parables of Jesus, the Christian graces, and various figures and legends of the Bible. The coloring of the whole is subdued and harmonious.

A painting class in College of Architecture.

Frank K. Foss '17 does the handstand as he trains for Olympic pole-vault championship (1920) and a world's record, 13 ft. 5⅛ in.

Senior singing at Schoellkopf Field.

Spring Day Carnival on Schoellkopf Field.

Thomas Frederick Crane (*left*). "From the organization of the University until his death in 1927, as Professor, Dean, Acting President, 'Tee-Fee' was as much a part of the Cornell scene as the Campus elms." David Fletcher Hoy '91 (*right*). "As Registrar and Secretary of the Committee on Student Conduct. 'Davy' was, for nearly forty years, the administrative officer of the University who dealt with students most frequently and intimately."

S. H. (Hibby) Ayer '14, the hula-hula girl, receiving instruction in cheerleading from an undergraduate. Hibby wrote the song, "Cornell Victorious."

(1910's) 75

The 1920's

President Schurman's resignation took effect in June 1920, after one of the longest Presidential terms on record, during which Cornell had grown from a small institution of 1700 students and a Faculty of 123 to more than 6000 students and some 890 Faculty members. It was a period in which many new and highly important changes were made in administration and organization, some of which were radical. New buildings were erected in rapid succession, particularly in the State College of Agriculture, and the boundaries of the University were extended from 370 to 1378 acres.

Albert W. Smith '78, Dean of Sibley College, was selected by the Trustees as acting President and held the office for sixteen months, until Dr. Livingston Farrand became the fourth President of the University.

President Farrand was graduated at the College of New Jersey (Princeton) in 1888 and received the MD in 1891 at Columbia, where he later held the chair of anthropology. He was president of University of Colorado for three years and then was chairman of the central committee, American Red Cross. He was fitted by temperament and training for a college presidency. He had the gift of liking and being liked by all. He was an excellent speaker on any occasion, whether to students, business men, or scientists. He guided the University with clear vision during an extremely difficult sixteen years (1921–37). A great achievement of his administration was the organization and administration of an imposing medical complex in New York City. The New York Hospital–Cornell Medical Center.

President Livingston Farrand.

George F. Baker, many times benefactor of Cornell, laying the cornerstone of Baker Laboratory of Chemistry.

The "Poughkeepsie Regatta" was at Ithaca in 1920. 30,000 spectators were massed on the hills, in grandstands, along the roads and Lake shore, and in boats at the finish. About 3500 cars visited Ithaca. The Varsity eight, after leading more than halfway, was beaten by Syracuse in a driving finish. Columbia was third; Penn, fourth. Time 11:02⅗.

Finish of an intercollege race on Cayuga Lake; Agriculture beats Arts by one-half length, "the usual hammer-and-tongs battle."

Freshman race on Cayuga Lake. Freshman 1923 crew, one of the best, beat the time of the varsity race in 10 min. 45⅖ sec.

Cornell History Club, 1921. *Seated:* Profs. J. P. Bretz, Nathaniel Schmidt, G. L. Burr '81, C. H. Hull '86, Blanche Hazard, William Westermann, C. L. Becker. *Standing:* E. W. Nelson PhD '23, G. C. Andrews PhD '20, W. B. Graves '21, E. H. Riley '15, Prof. Wallace Notestein, N. M. Crouse, Gussie E. Gaskill, L. R. Gottschalk '19, Harold Hulme PhD '25.

First class in Hotel Administration, 1922. *From left. Front:* H. M. Zinram '25, J. Dockery '25, Prof. Cornelius Betten PhD '06 (Vice-dean Agriculture), Prof. H. B. Meek, A. L. Olsen '25, A. Lang '26. *Row 2:* J. F. Hamil '26, H. P. Gun-'26, R. H. Boggs '26, L. G. Gibbs '26. dersdorf '25, K. M. Wilson '25, H. Merchand '25, A. W. Dunlap '25, C. A. Jennings '25. *Back rows:* C. L. Hanlon '26, A. P. Hanlon '26, J. H. Platt '26, J. M. Crandall '25, J. H. Courtney '25, W. H. Lodge '27, L. H. Combs '26, A. V. Taft

Coach John F. Moakley in action: the old standing jump.

Staff of the Cornell Alumni News, 1924. *From left. Front:* Prof. Clark S. Northup '93, Romeyn Berry '04, Florence Baker, R. W. Sailor '07, Prof. Bristow Adams. *Middle:* H. A. Stevenson '19, Harry G. Stutz '07, George M. Horton, Foster M. Coffin '12. *Back:* Laurence B. June '19, Barrett L. Crandall '13.

Acting President Albert W. ("Uncle Pete") Smith '78.

Baseball Coach John P. Henry (*left*), Advisory Coach Hugh Jennings '04, and the new (1919) Graduate Manager of Athletics, Romeyn Berry '04.

Baseball at Hoy Field in 1921: Yale 4, Cornell 1.

"When Knighthood Was In Flower," Spring Day 1923.

"Venice" *a la* Beebe Lake, Spring Day 1925.

First track meet in the Drill Hall. The curved line across the lanes marked the eight-lap-to-the-mile unbanked track. Pictured is the start of the final heat of the 70-yard hurdles, won by Carl Johnson of Michigan (7⅗ sec.). Score of the meet Cornell 45, Michigan (Conference champions) 40.

Class of '22 winners of women's baseball championship. *Standing:* Cornelia Walker, Lucille Knight, Genevieve Chambers, Charlotte Bacon, Alda Little. *Seated:* Rodney Mason, Gertrude Lynahan, Ellarene Hainsworth, Bertha Funnell, Marion McMillan.

Girls' interclass basketball in Old Armory.

In a 1921 cross-country race at Syracuse against Syracuse, MIT, Yale, Dartmouth, Colgate & Columbia, four Cornell runners crossed the finish-line abreast in record time: Capt. Charles C. Carter, Robert E. Brown, Norman P. Brown & George Miske. In the Intercollegiate race at New York the same four runners finished 1, 2, 3 & 5 with the unprecedented score of 18 in the largest field of runners on record.

The 1921 championship cross-country team. *From left. Seated:* G. Miske '22, R. E. Brown '22, Capt. C. C. Carter '22, N. P. Brown '22, C. G. Irish '23, E. A. Gordon '22. *Standing:* Asst. Mgr. R. J. Parker '23, H. Greenberg '22, G. C. Williams '24, Asst. Coach J. R. Bangs Jr. '21, Coach J. F. Moakley, M. J. Ward '23, J. Vandervort Jr. '22, Mgr. P. Johnson '22.

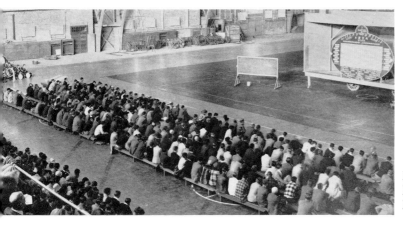

Football game returns on the Gridgraph in Drill Hall. Lights on the board were supplemented by Prof. "Bull" Durham's stentorian reading of telegraphed details.

Junior Week basketball game in Drill (Barton) Hall Feb. 14, 1920: Cornell 25, Yale 23.

ROTC Field Artillery: Above Cayuga Lake.

On Alumni Field.

Faculty veterans (*from left*): Dean Eugene E. Haskell '79, Professors Emeriti John L. Stone '74, George S. Moler '75 & Anna B. Comstock '85, Dean T. Frederick Crane, Prof. George L. Burr '81. Leading are Faculty Marshals Charles L. Durham '99 and Arthur W. Browne '03.

Oxford-Cambridge lacrosse team defeats Varsity 5–2.

Track teams at Princeton: Oxford-Cambridge 9½, Cornell-Princeton 2⅔; only first places scored.

1922 wrestling team regained Intercollegiates championship held by Cornell from 1910–18. *From left. Seated:* H. A. Roberts '23, W. D. Wright '23, Capt. R. S. Ackerly '22, L. C. Hanson '23, G. H. Freer '23. *Standing:* R. C. Ayau '24, Mgr. L. W. Hoyt '22, Coach W. C. O'Connell '11, E V. Strack '22, W. J. Wigsten '23. In 1920 Ackerly was the first American to win an Olympic championship in wrestling.

Joseph A. Lazarus '25, holder of University flyweight and bantamweight championships for four years; member of US Olympic team in 1926.

Gilmour Dobie, football coach 1920–36. In 1920 his team had six victories and two defeats and for the next three years they were undefeated and untied. In his sixteen years Cornell won eighty-two and tied seven of the 125 games played. *Right:* Capt. Edgar L. Kaw '23 getting off one of his famous punts. He was highest individual point-winner in the East and for two successive years a choice for All-American.

Class Reunions luncheon in Barton Hall, June 1925.

Swimming hole in upper Beebe Lake before the Henry W. Sackett '75 Bridge was built.

Women's rifle squad had "just completed a successful season in the intercollegiate competition."

University Commencement in Bailey Hall.

Spring Day Cosmopolitan Club show, representing many nations.

Polo, Cornell vs. Princeton, upper Alumni Field.

Underclass mud-rush, abolished in 1936; captives at right.

Louis Agassiz Fuertes '97 in his studio and with a trained duckhawk. His genius in the portrayal of birds has probably never been surpassed. His industry and accomplishments were astonishing; his sincerity and warm human sympathies, with his gifts of song and story, made him welcome at many gatherings.

Dr. Erl A. Bates, Adviser in Indian Extension, with a group of visitors.

Pontifex Maximus: Prof. "Bull" Durham '99 proclaims Nero's Birthday.

Between classes in spring.

Chariot race ending Spring Day Roman Circus.

Intramural games on upper Alumni Field. Crescent added to Schoellkopf Stadium in 1924 provides some 20,000 seats.

Spring Day "peerade": Architects in huge dragon writhe in and out before the watching crowd.

The enlarged Johnny Parson Club on the coast of Beebe Lake, with store, restaurant, check room for skaters, hockey room, and open fireplace.

Silent sentinels wrapt in reveries.

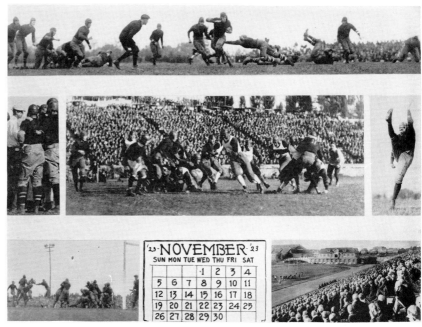

A page of a (John P.) Troy Calendar.

Yacht "Carlsark" and crew of J. E. Estabrook '32, F. P. Kneen '29, Captain-owner C. L. Weagant '29, D. N. Schoales '29, J. M. Rummler '29 made a cruise of a year and 13,000

miles to the Mediterranean and island of Ithaca, Greece, where they climbed Mt. Aitos, ancient home of Ulysses, and left a marble tablet inscribed, "Cornell Forever."

In 1927 Cornell won the coveted Intercollegiates foils championship, defeating Army, Yale, Columbia, Navy, Pennsylvania. *From left. Seated:* S. S. Robbins '28, Capt. Fernando Chardon '28, Coach Francis Darrieulat, Earl Good '28. *Standing:* P. P. Pirone '28, M. L. Smith '29, J. M. Pulvino '27, Mgr. A. H. Church '28.

Henry A. Russell '26 equalling the world's record in the 220-yard dash (20⅖ sec.) at MIT meet. As a Senior he won the 100- and 220-yard dash in every meet, including Intercollegiates and Oxford-Cambridge. He set a world record for the 75-yard indoors and a new Intercollegiates for the 220 outdoors (20⅕ sec.) and he equalled the Intercollegiates 100-yard record (9⁷⁄₁₀ sec.).

"The Straight" main entrance.

Willard Straight Hall, given by Mrs. Leonard K. Elmhirst in memory of her first husband, Willard D. Straight '01, who wished that his estate might "serve in some way to enrich student life and to enlarge the opportunities for human contact at his Alma Mater." The building was designed for all activities other than athletics.

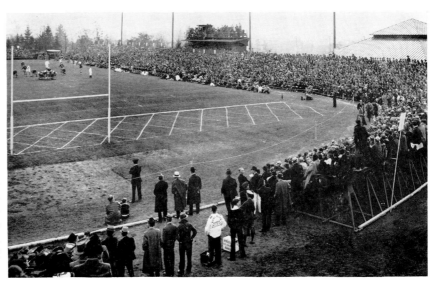

Cornell 24, Dartmouth 23: a classic in Cornell football annals. "The 25,000 persons who filled the Crescent, who screamed, wept, fainted, and burst blood-vessels when Carey kicked the field-goal in the last minute of play had the privilege of witnessing a miracle." The Red Eleven had been 16 points behind when the final period of this 1926 game opened.

Original west terrace of Willard Straight Hall. Enclosed, it was a World War II Army mess hall and is now the popular Ivy Room.

Willard Straight Memorial Room.

President Livingston Farrand shows Sao-Ke Alfred Sze '01, Chinese Minister to the US, and Robert E. Treman '09, chairman of the War Memorial committee, where Cornell's World War I Memorial will rise.

World War I Memorial and men's dormitory towers: McFaddin Hall at left, Lyon Hall at right. Top floor at right provides a meeting lodge for Quill & Dagger Society in recognition of its gift of $75,000 toward the building.

Colonade of the War Memorial.

The 1930's

This decade opened with the largest registration in the University's history (6246), an increase which was made in the face of hard times and higher entrance requirements, and which indicated, as the Cornell Alumni News wisely commented, "an increased capacity on the part of the University to properly teach properly prepared students."

With the new architecture that had come into vogue and greater attention given to landscaping, the Campus assumed a "new look" more than ever in harmony with its beautiful surroundings. With happy thought, Col. Henry W. Sackett '75 had provided $200,000 for landscaping the Campus, particularly Fall Creek and Cascadilla Creek gorges, and before his death in 1929 he had the satisfaction of seeing a considerable part of this work near completion.

Prof. Arthur A. Allen '08, Ornithology, gets an electric-earful of bird songs in the Florida palmetto jungle.

Henry W. Sackett ('75) Bridge at Beebe Lake, with bronze plaque.

Lua A. Minns ('14) Memorial Garden, with Dean Bailey's model schoolhouse and Bailey Hall at rear. (This is the present site of Malott Hall for the Graduate School of Business & Public Administration.)

Martha Van Rensselaer Hall houses the New York State College of Home Economics. The Department of Home Economics was organized in 1907 with Miss Van Rensselaer and Flora Rose as heads. They were appointed professors and were the first women given a vote in the Faculty. Together they developed the work in both resident and extension teaching. Some interesting laboratory work of the College is shown on these two pages.

Furniture built and repaired.

Automobile maintenance.

Household plumbing.

Dressmaking.

Martha Van Rensselaer was designated by the National League of Women Voters one of the twelve greatest living American women.

Sewing machines reconditioned.

Weaving.

The New York Hospital–Cornell University Medical Center occupies several city blocks above 68th Street along York Avenue in Manhattan. The group, designed to last a cen-tury, embodies the latest design and equipment for treat-ment and study of disease. Its original plan called for expenditure of $11,000,000 for buildings exclusive of land.

A meeting of a special committee of the Cornell Alumni Corporation. *From left:* T. S. Berna '12, F. M. Coffin '12, A. J. Whinery '10, E. J. Murphy '22, A. P. Bryant '99, C. A. Taussig '02, C. Van Blarcom '08, C. W. Wilson '00, R. E. Tre-man '09, F. S. Winslow '06, J. A. Pollock '07, K. W. Gass '12, T. I. S. Boak '14.

Polo players A. Nathalie Colvocoresses '38 and Anne M. Simpson '36.

Women's Riding Club. *From left:* Helena Browne '32, Margaret Hapgood '30, Martha Williams '32, Mary Wood '30, M. Louise Stevens '32, Isabelle Thro '31.

First winners of scholarships given by the Federation of Cornell Women's Clubs (all Class of '37). *From left:* Flora W. Daniel, Grace H. Jones, Doris E. Smallridge, Esther M. Dillenbeck, Beth W. Dawson.

Fuertes Observatory north of Beebe Lake. "On Friday nights, when open to the public, this building is filled with Faculty, townspeople, and children; star-gazers all."

The Faculty in 1932 consisted of 373 professors and assistant professors resident in Ithaca. Student registration was 5394.

Trustees Jacob F. Schoellkopf '05 and Myron C. Taylor '94 with Public Information Director Louis C. Boochever '12 in doorway of Morrill Hall. Descending steps are Trustees Robert H. Treman '78, J. DuPratt White '90, and Chairman Frank H. Hiscock '75.

The Campus and vicinity in the early thirties. *Lower left:* Baker Dormitories and War Memorial. *Upper left:* Balch Halls for women. *Upper right center:* Plant Science Building. *Lower right:* New home of the Law School made possible by a gift of $1,500,000 from Myron C. Taylor '94.

Meeting of the University Administrative Committee in Morrill Hall. *From left. Seated:* Registrar E. F. Bradford, Treasurer G. F. Rogalsky '07, Provost A. R. Mann '04, President Livingston Farrand, Manager of Residential Halls Anna F. Grace '10, Comptroller C. D. Bostwick '92, Secretary Woodford Patterson '95. *Standing:* Director of Publicity L. C. Boochever '12, Legal Assistant L. N. Simmons '12, Alumni Representative F. M. Coffin '12, Auditor J. B. Trousdale '22, Manager of Purchases G. S. Frank '11, Superintendent of Buildings & Grounds C. VanBlarcom '08.

In April, 1930, the Women's Athletic Association conducted walking contests and trips to various points about Ithaca. Outstanding walker of the University proved to be Elizabeth H. A. vanLoben Sels MS '32, who won first prize for fifty miles at average of 4½ miles an hour. Tied for first in another contest were Yolanda J. Elsasser '32 and Jessie K. Lidell '32, who walked fifty-two miles on two Sundays. Shorter walks were conducted to the State Game Farm, Esty's Glen, Remington Salt Plant, Turkey Hill, Taughannock Falls, Enfield Glen, and Buttermilk Falls. Pictures on these two pages show walkers in Enfield Glen, now Robert H. Treman ('78) State Park, and waterfalls.

Ithaca Falls (90 feet high) in Fall Creek.

Taughannock Falls (215 ft.), highest east of Rockies.

Lucifer Falls, Enfield Glen.

Cornell Chinese Club.

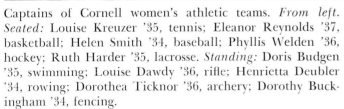

All out for lacrosse!

Captains of Cornell women's athletic teams. *From left.*
Seated: Louise Kreuzer '35, tennis; Eleanor Reynolds '37,
basketball; Helen Smith '34, baseball; Phyllis Welden '36,
hockey; Ruth Harder '35, lacrosse. *Standing:* Doris Budgen
'35, swimming; Louise Dawdy '36, rifle; Henrietta Deubler
'34, rowing; Dorothea Ticknor '36, archery; Dorothy Buck-
ingham '34, fencing.

The last observation train from Ithaca, 1936. Cayuga Lake
was rough all day; at 8 p.m. the crew races were cancelled.

At the 1934 Penn Relays this team of R. E. Linders '36, J. L. Messersmith '36, R. J. Kane '34, and R. A. Scallan '36 won the 880-yard race in 1 min. 27.8 sec. This and winning 440-yard and shuttle-hurdles teams were Cornell's first Relays victories since 1922.

Frank Sheehan, "the Irish philosopher," retired after forty years of ministering to Cornell athletes. Beginning as custodian of Percy Field and rubber at $6 a week, he mowed the grass, rolled the track, cleaned the clubhouse, did the laundry, and rubbed the athletes. He helped the 1920 American Olympic track team, coached by John F. Moakley, to victory in Antwerp and visited London and Dublin. A Cornell Alumni News chronicler reported: "He didn't bring back any Guinness Stout from Dublin, but damit he might just as well have because they didn't look in his trunk; just lifted the lid and sez that's all right Frank. He met the King in London, but he didn't get a chance to bake him because the King was feelin' fine as it was."

Prof. Lyman P. Wilson holds moot court in Myron Taylor Hall.

Mount Pleasant Lodge east of Campus was erected under auspices of the WPA. *Right:* Week-end student party there.

Cornell was reproved in the message that accompanied this picture: "Gentlemen: Please deliver this picture to the two cultured and refined young ladies of Co-Educational Department of the University.—Mrs. A. M. C."

Ornithology Laboratory in McGraw Hall with Prof. Arthur A. Allen '08.

Southern ladies of the University in authentic *ante bellum* costumes celebrate the birthday of Robert E. Lee, entertaining 150 guests. *From left:* Mrs. J. D. Burfoot (Virginia), Mimi Barrows (Georgia), Mrs. Claire Granel (South Carolina), Geraldine Mason '39 (West Virginia), Nellie Tidline MS '37 (Virginia), Mrs. E. K. Graham PhD '34 (North Carolina).

"Floradora Sextet": Women's Glee Club members, with escorts.

University Board of Trustees after a meeting in Morrill Hall. *From left. Front:* R. B. Williams '01, J. DuPratt White '90, Dr. Mary M. Crawford '04, C. W. Pound '87, Mynderse Van Cleef '74, C. E. Cornell, P. Graves, President Livingston Farrand, F. H. Hiscock '75, R. H. Treman '78, E. B. Whitman '01. *Middle:* H. R. Ickelheimer '88, J. W. Parker '08, C. D. Bostwick '92, R. E. Treman '09. H. E. Babcock, P. G. Ten Eyck, E. T. Turner '83, J. F. Schoellkopf '05, Herman Diederichs '97, J. T. Newman '75, G. R. VanNamee '01, J. B. Tuck '93. *Back:* A. R. Mann '04, E. N. Sanderson '87, Ernest Merritt '86, M. M. Upson '99, M. C. Burritt '08, B. Pyrke, F. E. Gannett '98, Stanton Griffiths '10, A. D. Warner Jr. '00, Bancroft Gherardi Jr. '93,

Junior Week "Time Capsule" and its sponsors. Query: Was it buried? Douglas B. Blackburn '39 (*left*), chairman, Junior Week promotion committee; William T. Mills '39, president of Atmos, honor society that provided the capsule; Sidney N. Phelps '39 (*right*).

President Edmund E. Day speaks to Cornell Day for Women audience in Prudence Risley Hall dining room.

Speakers at Inauguration of President Edmund E. Day October 8, 1937. *From left. Front:* Presidents Ruthven of Michigan, Conant of Harvard, Day of Cornell, Hopkins of Dartmouth. *Back:* Governor Herbert H. Lehman, Trustee Chairman Frank H. Hiscock '75, Former Presidents Farrand and Schurman, Prof. C. L. Durham '99, master of ceremonies.

Home Economics Director Flora Rose and President Edmund E. Day escort Mrs. Franklin D. Roosevelt at Farm & Home Week.

Edmund Ezra Day, fifth President of Cornell; graduate of Dartmouth '05, professor at Harvard, dean of School of Business Administration at University of Michigan, Director for the School of Social Sciences of Rockefeller Foundation.

President Day speaks to Cornell Club of Rochester. *At left:* Mayor Samuel B. Dicker '11, Trustee Frank E. Gannett '98. *At right:* Club Presidents George A. West '23 and Mrs. Edwin K. Haas '32.

Prof. James E. Rice '90, head of Poultry Husbandry for thirty years, begins new career shaping policies and practices in poultry production.

Big Red Band on Schoellkopf Field.

M. Rosenbeck '39, R. N. Williams '38, S. S. Kilkenny Jr. '39. T. M. Smith '39 & C. H. Sheely '39 in Willard Straight Hall Game Room won Intercollegiate telegraphic straight-rail billiards championship in 1938 with score of 399. Cornell had also won in 1937 with score of 442, the highest thus far recorded.

Law School Library in Boardman Hall used from 1892–1932, with Librarian E. E. Willever.

Ivy League track & field champions 1939; first Cornell winners in five years of the Heptagonal Games. *From left. Front:* A. F. VanRanst '39, J. E. Rutledge '39, A. T. Davis III '39, J. H. Nevius '39, Capt. W. W. McKeever '39, J. B. Pender '39, M. J. Breitenbach '39, N. E. Dorius '39, J. C. Tallman '39. *Middle:* Asst. Coach J. R. Bangs Jr. '21, W. W. Zittel Jr. Murck '40, Asst. Coach E. G. Ratkoski '35.

'40, F. W. West Jr. '41, G. E. Ranney '39, E. G. Wingerter '40, D. A. Weadon '40, L. W. Wheeler '40, J. S. Hall '39, A. E. Walker Jr. '41, Coach John F. Moakley. *Back:* Mgr. L. H. Stevens '39, N. E. White '41, M. L. Urbanowitz '41, G. M. Walker '40, E. S. Washburn '40, W. McCutchen '40, R. W. Pressing '40, M. G. Olinger '39, Asst. Mgr. E. C.

In the middle '30's financial difficulties brought about reorganization of the Athletic Association and its somewhat anomalous relation to the University. James Lynah '05, retired industrialist and a former captain of the football team, was given Faculty rank as Director of Physical Education & Athletics and empowered to make needed changes. In his six years of service he achieved important results.

On the resignation of Coach Gilmour Dobie after sixteen years at Cornell, Carl Snavely, becoming head football coach with a new staff, was able to reverse the tides of defeat. Lynah selected as his assistant Henry S. Godshall Jr. '36, who was succeeded by Robert J. Kane '34, former track athlete and assistant to Coach Moakley; now Director of Physical Education & Athletics.

Cheerleaders doing their stuff.

Trainer Frank Kavanagh leads a new wrinkle in football training.

Dedication of memorial plaque to John McMullen, donor of John McMullen Scholarship Fund which has grown to more than $6,000,000 endowing scholarships "for young men in Engineering." Speakers standing just behind the plaque were Dean Emeritus Dexter Kimball, President Edmund E. Day, DeWitt D. Barlow (president of Atlantic Gulf & Pacific Co. which McMullen founded), and Dean S. C. Hollister. Others McMullen Regional Scholars from twenty-six States.

Women's fencing team. *From left:* Coach Georges Cointe, Ruth Howell '40, Jeannette Lehde '41, Geraldine Mason '39, Constance Eberhart '41.

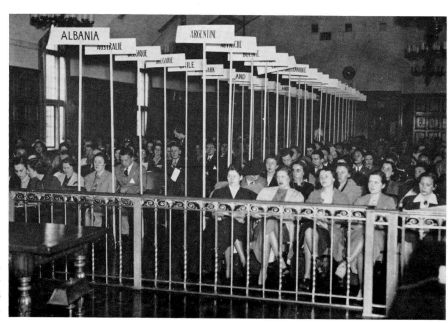

Model League of Nations, with delegates from thirty-six Eastern colleges and universities representing most countries of the world, meets in Moot Court Room of Myron Taylor Hall.

New interest in skiing. *From left. Front:* Esther Dillenbeck '37, Ruth Ryerson '35, Norma Nordstrom '35, Alice Bailey '36. *Back:* Margaret Kincaid '37, Marjorie Kane '36, Sara Wilder '36, Eleanor Middleton '35, Virginia Lauder '35, Doris Struss '35, Anne Allen '36, Marion Ganzenmuller '34.

Roller skating in Old Armory.

Westward down the slope from Willard Straight Hall showing Sigma Phi and Psi Upsilon fraternity houses; Mess Halls and McFaddin Hall and World War I Memorial at right.

Ezra Cornell and Quadrangle in winter garb.

"Too much snow; let's go skating!"

110 (1930's)

The 1940's

H. E. Babcock, Trustee chairman, John M. Olin '13, and President Edmund E. Day. Franklin W. Olin '75 gave $700,000 for construction of Olin Hall in memory of his elder son, Franklin W. Olin Jr. '12: first of the new Engineering College Quadrangle at south edge of Campus.

In the Second World War Cornell, with its military traditions, equipment, and established courses of elementary training, was transformed into an improvised military and naval academy.

In addition to directing this transformation, President Edmund E. Day attended frequent meetings in Washington as chairman of a Federal Board of Education. Throughout these years new courses and methods of instruction were added, Faculty changes and additions multiplied, and costly building operations were rushed to completion. A new administration building (now Edmund Ezra Day Hall) and new service buildings became imperative. Among other buildings erected were Clara Dickson Hall for women, Olin Hall for Chemical Engineering, Savage Hall for the School of Nutrition, and a Laboratory of Nuclear Studies given by Floyd R. Newman '12. Temporary buildings were assigned to the new New York State School of Industrial & Labor Relations, the Graduate School of Business & Public Administration, and Graduate School of Aeronautical Engineering supplementing the Cornell Aeronautical Laboratory in Buffalo.

The New York Herald-Tribune did not overvalue President Day's work when it said: "The growth and development of Cornell University during the dozen years he devoted to it as President and Chancellor are an enduring tribute to his energy, vision, and the liberal tradition which he fostered."

Director Fred H. Rhodes PhD '14, School of Chemical & Metallurgical Engineering; Dean S. C. Hollister, College of Engineering; President Edmund E. Day; Hugh E. Weatherlow '06, Superintendent of Buildings & Grounds; and Grove A. Stanton '07 on site of Olin Hall.

Olin Hall of Chemical Engineering at Central Avenue & Campus Road, built 1941.

Temporary buildings erected on Sage Green for the State School of Industrial & Labor Relations. The Quonset hut was first occupied by the Navy, then by the Veterans Administration.

Candidates for Student Council stage an election parade.

Student officers in the Navy Training School practice flag signalling on Old Armory Green south of Olin Hall.

Obeying Beebe Lake rules?

War-time Diesel Engine Laboratories on the Old Armory Green housing machinery used by the Navy for training, then given to the University.

Three of 115 special Engineering "Cadettes" taught in the Forge Shop by Instructor G. A. ("Nig") Hill. Ida Dietz, Patricia Hopkins, Jane Condleton.

Old Suspension Bridge across Fall Creek.

Navy cadets march by Baker Dormitories and Quill & Dagger tower.

Parking lot at Tower Road & East Avenue (where Day Hall now stands). In foreground is Prof. Charles Babcock's house, first home built on the Campus. Across East Avenue are the Veterinary College and Barton Hall.

War-time class in military map making, leading to Army Map Service, with Prof. P. H. Underwood '07 at left.

An Army Quartermaster Corps field kitchen unit serves lunch on Alumni Field to ROTC instructors Capt. A. F. Bolger & Major R. L. Hoff '40, President Edmund E. Day, ROTC Commandant Col. Ralph Hospital, Provost Arthur S. Adams, Trustee George R. Pfann '24.

The view of facing page after completion in 1947 of Edmund Ezra Day Hall, University administration building.

Army and Navy officers inspect war-time training units on upper Alumni Field, across Tower Road from College of Agriculture buildings.

ROTC students on Barton Hall rifle range. *From left:* Alastair Nixon '44, G. A. Gallagher '44, George Hughes (armorer for twenty-six years), D. A. Warren '44, Melvin Cohen '44.

War-time commando training and physical build-up for everybody, directed by Georges Cointe (*far right*).

A war-time Commencement in Barton Hall; President Edmund E. Day presiding. East portal at rear.

President Day: "Academic Structure & Size."

Vetsburg at East Ithaca, family housing for veterans attending Cornell.

Stone bench placed on Campus by Prof. Goldwin Smith in 1871; now in front of Goldwin Smith Hall. The inscription "Above All Nations Is Humanity" was chosen as the motto of Cornell Cosmopolitan Club, later by its National Association and by the International Congress of Students. Alina Surmacka '46 from Poland (*seated*) and Elizabeth Kerr '43 of Ithaca.

Students at the Cosmopolitan Club. Donald C. Kerr '12, Counselor to Foreign Students, is second from right in second row up. As E. B. White '21 said: "An undergraduate can know on the Campus two men from Hawaii, a Cuban, a Turk, an Englishman from India, a Negro from New York, two farmers, three Swedes, a Quaker, five Southerners, a reindeer-butcher, a second lieutenant, a motorcyclist, and a lutist."

Probably the largest number of students from Siam ever attending an American University at one time.

Officers of Women's Athletic Association by the fireplace in Willard Straight Memorial Room. Sort them out! They include Blanche Bassette '43, golf; Helen Bernhard '43, tennis; Alice Buhsen '42, riding; Winona Chambers '42, badminton; Constance Eberhart '41, fencing; Elizabeth Francel '43, canoeing; Caryl Jennings '42, rifle; Grace Kreiger '41, fencing; Virginia MacArthur '44, field hockey; Marjorie Magaziner '42, skiing; Eileen McQuillin '41, volleyball; Louise Nordenholt '42, archery; Katharine Rogers '43, basketball; Beth Smiley '43, golf; Bernadine Sutton '43, baseball; Jeanette Trieber '43, figure skating.

Model United Nations session in Willard Straight Memorial Room. James G. Ming Ling '52 of Pieping presents resolutions of the Security Council. Alvin L. Arnold '49 presides, with Leonard Lehman '49. *At tables, from left:* Helene Hano '48 (Massachusetts), Henry Behn-Eschenburg '48 (Mexico), Charlotte Choper '48 (New Jersey), Bette McGrew '49 (Illinois), Howard E. Smith '50 (New York).

Crowded main reading room of the University Library, now completely remodelled as Uris Library for undergraduates.

Student enrollment of about 1700 in 1892 had more than quintupled by 1950.

Cornell Day alumni "chauffeurs" at Johnny Parson Club smoker.

Sunday afternoon Band concert on McGraw Hill slope.

Polo on upper Alumni Field.

Spring Day is here again: an act in Bailey Hall variety show and "peerade" float.

Theta Xi prize-winner in Junior Week ice sculpture.

Architects' Beaux Arts Ball, "Night on the Nile."

Tar Young Ski Hill at Caroline, ten miles east of Campus.

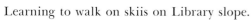

Learning to walk on skiis on Library slope.

Skiing instruction on Library slope.

Dormitories for women: Balch Halls upper right; Clara Dickson Hall under construction.

Charles Weidman and Doris Humphrey (*center*) give instruction in Old Armory to Modern Dance Club and guests from Wells, Elmira, and Syracuse before their Bailey Hall recital.

Mrs. E. M. Statler lays cornerstone of Statler Hall for School of Hotel Administration; Dean H. B. Meek and President E. E. Day assisting.

Main Statler Hall kitchen is inspected by Carlos Osuna '51 of Mexico and Norman R. Brown '53 of North Dakota.

Modern decorative scheme of the practice inn section carried out in main dining room of Statler Hall.

Hotel School "C" men in close finish of "Waiters' Derby": R. J. McDonald '38, R. B. MacNab '36, J. P. Floros '36, T. C. Burns '36, J. M. Batten '37.

Statler Hall, given by the Statler Foundation to house School of Hotel Administration, a thirty-six-room practice inn, and Statler Club for Faculty and staff members with lounges, (*below*), library, and dining-rooms.

"Waiters' Derbies" are not an official part of Hotel School training. Co-eds (*from left*): Joan Blaikie '45 (winner), Amy Mann '45, Jacqueline Rogers '46, Janice O'Donnell '44, Patricia Will '45, Joyce Heath '47.

Student fashion show of yesteryear. *From left:* Francis Wilson '46, Evelyn Carlson '46, Helen Paulus '48, Florence Dombrowski '48, Sue Jameson '45, Joan Kestor '48.

Student fashion show recalling "flappers" of the 1920's. *From left:* Matilda Norfleet '48, Barbara Pond '47, Ellen Flemming '48, Sally Robinson '46, Patricia Grabb '47, Margaret Schiavone '44.

Old Armory crew room in use fifty years; now replaced by rowing tanks in Teagle Hall. Coach R. H. (Stork) Sanford instructs.

Cornell honors its Nobel Prize winners. President Edmund E. Day presents scrolls at a Waldorf-Astoria dinner in New York: (*from left*) Isidor I. Rabi '19 (Physics, 1944), Prof. Peter J. Debye (Chemistry, 1938), Pearl S. Buck AM '25 (Literature, 1938), John R. Mott '88 (Peace, 1946), Gustav Nobel (founder's nephew), Prof. James B. Sumner (Chemistry, 1946). Not pictured is Prof. Vincent duVigneaud, Biochemistry at the Medical College, who received a Nobel Prize in 1955.

Prof. C. M. McCay, Nutrition, (*second from left*) received $2000 national award for year's best service in interest of dogs. Others from left are Dean W. A. Hagan MS '17, Veterinary; Prof. James S. Knapp '31 (*background*); award committee; Dean W. I. Myers '14, Agriculture.

Cornell Corinthian Yacht Club gives sailing instruction.

For a student orientation program, Faculty members plan a symposium on "The Impact of War on America." *From left:* Profs. Robert E. Cushman, Royal E. Montgomery, Cornelis W. deKiewiet, Knight Biggerstaff, Philip E. Mosely, Herbert W. Briggs.

Memorial service after World War II in front of World War I Memorial.

State College Deans William I. Myers '14 (Agriculture), Elizabeth L. Vincent (Home Economics), Acting President Cornelis W. de Kiewiet, and Dean William A. Hagan MS '17 (Veterinary) greet President Alvin C. Eurich (*center*) of State University of New York which includes the State Colleges at Cornell.

Sheila, seven months, was baby-in-residence in Home Economics practice apartment in 1948. Her temporary foster-mothers are Ruth Davidson '49 (*left*) and Grace Hubbell '49.

Tutor Marie Tolstoy gives blackboard lesson in Russian language to Joyce Edelstein '45, Olga Gallik '44, and Mary Rettger '42.

Selective Service examination in Baker Laboratory.

Twenty-five-year Reunion of 1924 Varsity basketball team. *From left. Seated:* F. D. Rossomondo '26, C. F. Wedell '24, C. H. Capron '24, M. L. Byron '24, M. L. Dake '26. *Standing:* J. D. Lincoln '24, G. R. Pfann '24, Coach H. B. Ortner '19, D. J. Post '24.

Class Reunion tents on Library slope.

Former Dean Dexter S. Kimball gets a memento at opening of the Kimball Room in Willard Straight Hall. President Warren G. Harms '50 and Director Foster M. Coffin '12 present it. Dean Kimball was an outstanding industrial organizer, introduced a new program of training into the engineering curricula of schools over the country. "Of broad human understanding, kindly humor, and deep loyalty to Cornell, he was known to innumerable alumni as a friend."

John F. Moakley, who spent fifty years coaching more than 4000 Cornellians, retired in 1949. In the fall of 1899 Moakley came to Cornell to begin a career that has had few equals in college athletics. Probably no other institution in the country has traditions in two sports equaling those bequeathed to Cornell by Charles E. Courtney in rowing and John F. Moakley in track. No one can measure the effects of such traditions upon the life of an institution or upon the lives and characters of the men they trained. Their records in victories are impressive, but much more important was the building of character in the students who came under the influence of these men of character and understanding.

A Faculty group. Now there were 362 professors, 243 associate professors, 172 assistant professors in Ithaca.

Classes move outdoors to the Quadrangle.

Eight-ton radio telescope, one of the earliest, follows sun automatically and records solar "noise." In background, a modified Army radar mount with 200-megacycle receiver making astronomical radio observations.

Fiftieth anniversary of Cornell Alumni News, 1949. *From left:* Managing Editor H. A. Stevenson '19, first Editor Clark S. Northup '93, Editor R. W. Sailor '07.

The 1950's

President Edmund E. Day resigned July 1, 1949, and was appointed Chancellor, with the larger interests of the University still in his hands. For reasons of health he was counselled to resign the Chancellorship January 31, 1950. As has appeared, the twelve years of his Presidency were a period of rapid growth in student enrollment and Faculty and in new schools and units, responsive to the diversified needs of a changing world. The physical developments kept pace with these new demands: buildings both permanent and temporary were constructed and plans were made for others.

From the Faculty Necrology of 1950: "The Cornell of Andrew D. White partook of his indomitable idealism; the Cornell of Jacob Gould Schurman shared his superb, almost restless energy; the Cornell of Livingston Farrand became somehow more urbane, more kindly, more human; the Cornell of Edmund Ezra Day became more socially conscious and more cognizant of its duties to the State and world."

Deane Waldo Malott was born in Abilene, Kans. in 1898. He was graduated at University of Kansas in 1921 and in 1923 he received the MBA at Harvard Business School, where he remained as assistant dean until 1929. After serving until 1933 as vice-president of the Hawaiian Pineapple Co. in Honolulu, he returned to Harvard Business School as associate professor and in 1939 was appointed chancellor of University of Kansas. He became the sixth President of Cornell University September 19, 1951, and served for twelve years.

President Deane W. Malott.

Olin Foundation in 1952 gave $2,549,000 to the Medical College in New York for a student dormitory, in memory of Franklin W. Olin '75. *From left:* James O. Wynn, vice-president Olin Foundation; Dean Joseph C. Hinsey of the Medical College; Trustee Neal D. Becker '05; Charles L. Horn, Olin Foundation president; President Deane W. Malott.

Members of Cornell's "American English" class for foreign students write their Season's Greetings in thirteen languages. Instructor Peter Holub stands second from right.

Installation of Deane W. Malott as the sixth President of Cornell.

In the One World Room of Anabel Taylor Hall, montage photographs of many lands make mural decorations.

An international group of women students. *From left:* Pauline Soong '52 of Shanghai, Jane Wigsten '50 of Horseheads, N.Y., Suad Walim '50 of Beirut, Lebanon, Margaret Yung '51 of Shanghai, Constance Semon '50 of Cuyahoga Falls, Ohio.

Dramatic Club in 1950 presented a bigger and better revival of the hilarious "Once Upon a Hill or What Happened in Mr. Cornell's Cow Pasture," written four years earlier by Walter Witcover '44, Priscilla A. Okie '45 & Virginia M. Genove '48. This tableau has the victorious Cornell crew of 1875 applauded by students with the Cornell Cheer that originated that "sunny summer morn" at Saratoga. Crew members in the play were R. J. Glavin Jr. '51, S. J. Tauber '52, J. E. Bostwick '53, P. T. Matthews '54, J. E. Pearl '54.

Prof. A. M. Drummond retired in 1952; since 1909 taught public speaking and directed the Dramatic Club.

Class of '51 officers of Women's Self Government Association help Santa Claus. *From left:* Karen Lamb, Mary Mundy, Martha Palmer (president), Margaret Dutcher (vice-president), Jean Eagle (secretary).

Myron Taylor Hall (Law School) and the new interfaith center, Anabel Taylor Hall (*right*). Both were gifts from

Myron C. Taylor '94, board chairman of U.S. Steel Co. who later represented American Presidents to the Vatican.

Myron C. Taylor '94 and Mrs. Taylor are greeted by President Deane W. Malott after dedication ceremonies of Anabel Taylor Hall, named for her. *Right:* Anabel Taylor

Hall, home of Cornell United Religious Work, has a mechanically interchangeable altar for Christian, Jewish, and inter-denominational services.

Charles H. Moore Jr. '51 set a world record (50.7 sec.) for the 400-meter hurdles at the 1952 Olympic Games at Helsinki, Finland.

World War II Memorial in Anabel Taylor Hall lobby. Carved stone tablet bears names of the 478 Cornellians who gave their lives. Black granite base has inscription from an 1865 letter by President Lincoln to a grieving mother: "So Costly a Sacrifice Upon the Altar of Freedom."

Spring football practice was abolished in 1952.

Letitia Ann Hays '52, named intercollegiate women's rifle champion by National Rifle Association, had a perfect score of 500.

Talking it over after the last exam.

Veterinary College graduates in 1950 with their families. Class of '50 had forty war veterans, eight non-veterans, one woman.

Big Red Band in Barton Hall.

Dinner in Willard Straight Hall celebrates Liberty
Hyde Bailey's ninetieth birthday six weeks late because on his birthday, March 15, 1948, he had been
collecting rare palms in the West Indian wilds. *From
left:* Jared VanWagenan Jr. '91, a student of Bailey's;
his daughter, Ethel Bailey Grad '11-'12; President Edmund E. Day; Prof. Bailey, Dean of Agriculture 1903-
12; Dean William I. Myers '14; Dean Elizabeth Lee
Vincent, Home Economics.

Prof. L. H. Bailey (1858–1955) at ninety-three in his Hori-
torium workshop adjoining his home on Sage Place.

Spring Day 1954: Cinderella prize float at right and Pogo in foreground.

Olympic medal winners 1952: Charles H. Moore Jr. '51, winner 400-meter hurdles; Meredith C. Gourdine '52, second in broad jump & Intercollegiates record 25 ft. 9¾ in.; Walter S. Ashbaugh '51, fourth in hop, step & jump.

Quadrangle of the State College of Agriculture, looking east to Albert R. Mann ('04) Library.

Dedication of Jack Moakley House. *From left:* Robert E. Treman '09, James Lynah '05, President Deane W. Malott, Coach John F. Moakley, Daniel A. Reed '98, John Paul Jones '13, Neal D. Becker '05, Robert J. Kane '34.

University golf course; George L. Hall, Varsity team coach since 1936, instructing.

Jack Moakley House at University Golf Course and cross-country course.

Teagle Hall, men's gymnasium, has a tunnel under Garden Avenue (*lower left*) from locker rooms to Barton Hall.

Walter C. Teagle '00 (*right*) and Mrs. Teagle present the key of Teagle Hall, new men's gymnasium they gave, to President Deane W. Malott and Trustee Board Chairman John L. Collyer '17.

Coach R. Harrison ("Stork") Sanford gives winter instruction in the rowing tank of Teagle Hall. Water flow can be regulated.

A diver takes off from the high board in Teagle Hall pool.

Old Armory, which The Cornell Sun in 1883 called "the finest Military and Gymnastic Hall in the country," was used as a women's gymnasium after Barton and Teagle Halls were built; then was demolished to make way for Hollister Hall, Civil Engineering.

Swimming Coach G. Scott Little checks starters for a Teagle Hall race.

Coach Georges L. Cointe instructs Philippe J. Mocquard '55 in Teagle Hall fencing room.

Coach Cointe with two of his champions. Philippe J. Mocquard '55 (*center*) won the 1954 Eastern Intercollegiate Fencing Association foil championship and was voted outstanding fencer of the year at the NCAA meet. Richard W. Pew '55 (*right*) was Eastern Intercollegiate epee champion, 1954 & 1955, and in the 1956 Olympic Games placed fourth in the epee finals, winning more bouts than any other contender.

Central Avenue.

Ivy League football champions, 1953. *From left. Front:* R. P. Zechman '54, A. N. D'Agostino '54, H. J. Bool '54, J. H. Gerdes '55, Capt. W. I. George '54, P. T. Kalinich '55, F. K. Hummel '54, J. A. Sebald '54, L. R. Walters '54, S. Tsapis '54. *Row 2:* A. J. Boyle '55, G. H. Bedrossian '55, J. F. Morris '55, R. E. Lewis '55, J. K. VanBuren '55, R. S. Mathewson '55, L. J. Oniskey '55, T. A. Marciniak '55, T. S. Rooney '55, D. J. Murphy '55, D. S. Kennedy '55. *Row 3:* G. R. Pfann Jr. '55, J. Marotta '55, R. C. Jackson '56, W. DeGraaf '56, E. F. Wilson '56, S. V. Intihar '56, R. T. DeStephano '55, J. D. Braun '55, J. P. Simon '55, E. R. Meade '56, D. F. Begin '56. *Row 4:* J. B. Talierco '56, J. R. Anderluh '56, F. R. Vadney '56, R. F. Stofle '56, W. J. Purdy '56, W. R. Forbes '55, N. L. Rowe '55, B. V. Brennan '56, W. Nevison '55, A. E. Brezinsky '55, F. J. Ripp '55. *Back:* J. Gorski '56, C. L. Glaser '55, R. W. Borland '56, J. R. Trueman '56, S. C. Alessi '54, R. S. Miller '56, A. W. Hall '56, J. K. Leighow '54, J. S. Hunt '56, D. P. Hoover '55.

Spring Day "boat race" on Beebe Lake ends in flames.

Entrance road to Cornell Plantations from Forest Home drive.

Preparing for test of space vehicle component at air speed up to 12,000 m.p.h. in Aeronautical Laboratory Wave Superheater Hypersonic Tunnel designed and built under U.S. Department of Defense sponsorship.

Part of the Cornell Aeronautical Laboratory in Buffalo, wholly owned research subsidiary of the University.

1954 cross country Heptagonals champions won four of their five dual meets. *From left. Front:* C. Trayford '55, J. J. Rosenbaum Jr. '56, Co-capts. D. T. Farley Jr. '55 & P. W. Loberg '55, M. J. Browne '55, H. E. Shearer Jr. '57. *Back:* Mgr. P. A. Bowell Jr. '55, R. H. Taft '56, A. Z. MacComber '55, R. D. Gosse '57, D. T. Secor Jr. '56, A. A. Patterson '57, Coach L. C. Montgomery.

Class Reunion luncheon in Barton Hall.

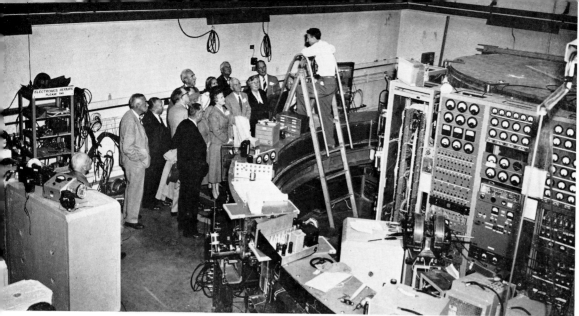

Prof. B. D. McDaniel PhD '43 explains to University Council members the cyclotron built in Newman Laboratory of Nuclear Studies; the Laboratory given by Floyd R. Newman '12.

Ellis L. Phillips '95, whose Phillips Foundation gave Phillips Hall for Electrical Engineering, holds switch to start dynamo (*at rear*) built at University for first permanent electric lighting system, to light plaque behind Mrs. Phillips and President Deane W. Malott. At left is Dean S. C. Hollister, Engineering.

Reunion sing at steps of Goldwin Smith Hall.

Albert W. Hall '56 practices at Schoellkopf Field. He set Cornell records for the outdoor hammer throw of 204 ft. 5½ in. and for the 35-pound weight indoors of 63 ft. 3¼ in.; won national AAU championships in both events several times; was a member of U.S. Olympic teams in 1956, 1960 & 1964.

1954–55 track team undefeated in dual meets and indoor & outdoor Heptagonal Games champions. *From left. Front:* N. H. Beachley '55, L. Lattomus '55, D. T. Farley Jr. '55, P. W. Loberg '55, Capt. A. Dadagian '55, R. A. Stanton '55, J. F. Morris '55, M. J. Browne '55. *Row 2:* Coach L. C. Montgomery, E. R. Mihm '57, P. L. Todd '56, J. J. Rosenbaum Jr. '56, H. E. Shearer Jr. '57, A. W. Hall '56, A. L. Boland Jr. '57, R. S. Abell '57, Asst. Coach E. G. Ratkoski '35. *Row 3:* Asst. Mgr. J. T. Ewers '56, G. P. Kendall '56, S. E. Betancourt '57, R. E. Lewis '55, F. Weicker Jr. '55, J. H. Marshall '55, R. M. Allman '57, Mgr. T. H. Arnott '55, Asst. Mgr. J. C. Mahlstedt '56. *Back:* Asst. Coach G. Gerlough, R. N. Zeitlin '57, W. S. Carpenter '57, R. A. Boice '56, R. T. Guelcher '56, W. S. LaLonde '55, D. Feldman '56, W. G. Gibson '57.

University Trustee William Littlewood '20 speaks in the Big Red Barn at a luncheon meeting of University Council members with student leaders.

Big Red Barn is alumni gathering place. President Andrew D. White's barn and carriage house is remodelled for informal meetings with gifts from alumni.

Sophomore Halfback Irvin (Bo) Roberson on his way for 74-yard touchdown run against Princeton at Schoellkopf Field. His attackers were blocked out by Roberson's '58 Classmates Christian Hatton (78) & Robert Blake (80). Roberson ran for 116 yards in ten carries that game.

Edgar L. Kaw '23 was first Cornellian elected to National Football Hall of Fame. He was All-American halfback on the undefeated teams of 1921 & 1922; receives his certificate from Athletic Director Robert J. Kane '34 on Schoellkopf Field in the presence of twenty-two former team-mates who came for the presentation.

Charles G. Rolles '56 broke all basketball scoring records. Only 5 ft. 6 in. and 140 pounds, the diminutive red-head calmly scored 1622 points in his four years of play; set a season record of 519 as a Senior & co-captain; achieved a high for Barton Hall of 37 against Brown in 1955; high score of 42 for any Varsity game and most field goals, 19, against Syracuse in 1956.

Three students gave alumni their frank evaluations of Cornell at a 1956 meeting of the University Council. Preparing here with Prof. Clinton L. Rossiter '39, Government, who introduced them, are (from left) Colin G. Campbell '57, Stanley R. Byron '54, Nancy J. Hecht '58.

Cornell crew beats Yale for the Grand Challenge Cup at Royal Regatta at Henley-on-Thames, England, July 6, 1957. The day before, in 23 seconds faster time of 6 min. 30 sec. for the mile-and-five-sixteenths course, Cornell led by a length the Russian champions, Krasnoe Znamia. A week later, competing against nine nations in the final race of a regatta at Lucerne, Switzerland, Cornell in a borrowed shell beat Italy's champion, the Motto Guzzi Rowing Club.

Collyer Boathouse was given by John L. Collyer '17 and Mrs. Collyer and he gave an equal gift of $200,000 in the Centennial campaign for athletic endowments and maintenance of the Boathouse. At left is pictured the old Boathouse given by the Class of '90, now replaced by a house for the coaching launches.

World championship Cornell crew of 1957 guests of honor at University Council dinner in Statler Hall ballroom. With but few changes this crew of '57 men had won four consecutive IRA championships, culminating with the Grand Challenge Cup at the Royal Henley Regatta in England. President Deane W. Malott congratulates Commodore C. W. Chapman, who rowed No. 6. Other crew members, from left, are P. T. Gravink, stroke; G. F. Ford, 7; W. J. Schumacher, 5; O. S. Simpson Jr., 4; D. F. Davis, 3; R. W. Staley, 2; C. W. Schwarz, coxswain; J. M. Van Horn, bow. Coach R. H. Sanford and volunteer trainer Georges Cointe flank the President. Toastmaster was Director of Athletics Robert J. Kane '34 (*right*).

Gannett Medical Clinic has in its lobby a portrait of Frank E. Gannett '98 and high on two sides (*see upper left*) murals by Mrs. Morris Bishop depicting Gannett's career as a Cornell student. The building, for student health services, was the gift of the Frank E. Gannett Newspaper Foundation.

Walter S. Carpenter Jr. '10 (*right*) gave Carpenter Hall for the administrative offices and library of the College of Engineering, for which he also gave an endowment. This picture is in the A. W. Smith Lounge for recreational reading, just off the Engineering Library, with portrait of Dean Albert W. ("Uncle Pete") Smith '78. Carpenter is with Dean Smith's widow, Prof. Ruby Green Smith PhD '14, and Dean S. C. Hollister, whom he credited with the principal responsibility for conceiving and carrying out the "tremendous new concept" of the College and its quadrangle of modern buildings at the south edge of the Campus (see p. 159).

vonCramm Hall on University Avenue just below Stewart Avenue is the University's first scholarship residence for students. It is named for Baron Friederich S. vonCramm, who was killed in 1941 in the German Army; came from a gift of $300,000 through T. B. Gilchrist '06, who was administrator of the Baron's mother's estate.

Prof. D. Keith Falkner taught singing in the Music Department for ten years before he became in June 1960 director of the Royal College of Music in London, England. With accompanist Robert Burns Meikle, Grad, he directs (*from left*) Carol B. Scott '61, Carol Elder of Ithaca, Barbara L. Federer '62, Rosalee Szabo '60, Lai Seng Yeoh '60.

Playing fields and new athletic facilities. Built into Upper Alumni Field just east of Teagle Hall (see p. 141) is Lynah Skating Rink, named for James Lynah '05, late Director of Physical Education & Athletics. At center, between Bacon Cage and Teagle Hall, is Grumman Squash Courts building, gift of Leroy R. Grumman '16, which also has a football ticket office. Hoy Field and Schoellkopf Field are in foreground.

Lynah Rink, with 85 by 200 feet of artificial ice and seats for 4200 spectators, is responsible for fervent interest in intercollegiate and "peewee" hockey, skating for all the community, and figure skating instruction from mid-November to early March.

Alice Statler Auditorium, a completely equipped theater with 920 seats, is in a new south wing of Statler Hall for which the Statler Foundation added to its previous gifts $2,300,000. Besides the auditorium named for Mrs. E. M. Statler, board chairman of the Foundation, this wing has in its five floors a larger library, lecture room, laboratories, class rooms, student lounge, exhibit room, and Faculty offices for the School of Hotel Administration. The Statler Foundation built and endowed Statler Hall and has endowed E. M. Statler Scholarships and made other gifts to the Hotel School.

Cornell's first Eastern Intercollegiate Fencing Association epee champions, 1958. *Seated:* Coach Georges L. Cointe, R. T. Thomas '57. *Standing:* J. H. Wiley '59, R. B. Cole '58.

Dean S. C. Hollister speaks at dedication of Upson Hall. Maxwell M. Upson '99, seated second from right next to President Malott, gave the building for the School of Mechanical Engineering. Other gifts to the University and Upson's announcement for the Centennial campaign that he had bequeathed $8,500,000 and $500,000 more for the Medical College in New York would make his total gifts to Cornell $10,840,000, the most from any benefactor. Other speakers at Upson Hall dedication were (*from left*) the Rev. Glenn A. Olds, Director of CURW; Director Harry J. Loberg '29, Mechanical Engineering; Richard G. Brandenburg '58.

Willard Straight Hall gets new director. Foster M. Coffin '12 (*left*) Director of the Straight since May 1925, before it opened, retired June 30, 1958, and turned over its management to Edgar A. Whiting '29, who was Coffin's assistant since 1930.

John S. King '58 twice won the Heptagonal Games high jump, setting a new indoor record of 6 ft. 8½ in. in 1958. In 1957 he won the Games broad jump outdoors.

College of Agriculture Alumni Association past-presidents gather at fiftieth anniversary. *From left. Seated:* T. E. La-Mont '27, D. J. Wickham '24, M. B. Galbreath '26, the first president in 1909 Jared Van Wagenen Jr. '91, R. F. Fricke '17, E. V. Underwood '13, A. W. Gibson '17. *Standing:* L. E. Curtis '35, W. H. Sherman '35, P. J. McManus '32, J. H. Pendergast '38, H. J. Evans '17, J. R. Hazlitt '24, J. P. King '36, M. Adams '33.

1958 wrestling team, undefeated Ivy League champions, win Eastern Intercollegiate Wrestling Association title first time in twenty-eight years. Among sixteen competitors Cornell scored 64 against Lehigh 49, Syracuse 45, Penn State 35, Pittsburgh 27. Capt. R. F. Vincent '58 kneels with trophy. Others, from left: J. E. Carter '60, R. W. Fillius '59, D. C. Auble '60, J M. Gardner Jr. '59, C. J. Molino '58, D. R. Dunlop '59, S. Friedman '59.

David C. Auble '60, Varsity wrestler at 123 pounds, was never defeated in a dual meet; was Eastern Intercollegiate Wrestling Association champion 1958, 1959, 1960, & NCAA champion twice; took fourth place for U.S. in 1964 Olympic Games in freestyle at 125.5 pounds.

First meeting of advisory Cornell Law School Council, October 1958. *From left. Seated:* R. S. Wilkins, Dean Gray Thoron, Chairman F. S. Wood '23, W. P. Rogers LLB '37, J. Weintraub '28, R. E. Coulson '09. *Standing:* L. W. Dawson '19, W. C. O'Brien '21, R. J. McDonald '38, F. B. Ingersoll '17, J. D. Bennett '33, A. M. Saperston '19, F. C. Heath LLB '37, Associate Dean W. D. Curtiss '38.

Prof. W. A. Campbell, Music, started in 1953 Band Days for high school musicians who are invited to play together at a football game each fall on Schoellkopf Field. The occasion now attracts some 5000 youngsters in 75 bands.

Humanities Council of College of Arts & Sciences studies common problems of related divisions. *From left:* Profs. J. M. Cowan, Linguistics; E. A. Blackall, German Literature; M. H. Abrams, English; M. G. Bishop '14, Romance Literature; J. A. Mazzeo, English & Italian; Chairman S. M. Brown Jr. '37, Philosophy; G. M. Kirkwood MA '39, Classics; F. O. Waage, Fine Arts; H. D. Albright PhD '36, Speech & Drama; F. E. Mineka, English; D. J. Grout, Music.

Hollister Hall for School of Civil Engineering is named for Prof. S. C. Hollister (*left*), Dean of Engineering 1937–59. Spencer T. Olin '21, pictured with Mrs. Olin, gave the $2,000,000 building and $500,000 for equipment in memory of his father, Franklin W. Olin '86.

Dramatic Club notables celebrate fifty years from 1909. *From left:* Sidney Kingsley '28; Prof. G. A. McCalmon, University Theatre director; Dr. Smiley Blanton MD '14, first Club director; Prof. H. D. Albright PhD '36, former director; Julius Zieget '10, first president; Prof. Damon Boynton '31, former president; Prof. W. H. Stainton '19, former director.

Coach Carl Snavely lines up his famous 1940 football team nineteen years later. All are Class of '41. From left, in the line are Alvah E. Kelley Jr., Nicholas Drahos, Fred W. West Jr., Louis J. Conti, Frank K. Finneran, Walter J. Sickles, Kasimir E. Hipolit. Backs: William J. Murphy Jr., Walter J. Matuzsak, Walter Scholl Jr., Harold F. McCullough.

The 1960's

Halfway in this decade, the University celebrated the Centennial of its Charter, which was granted by the New York State Legislature and signed by Governor Reuben E. Fenton April 27, 1865.

The twelve-year term of President Deane W. Malott ended with his retirement June 30, 1963 and the Trustees elected him President Emeritus. Professor Morris Bishop '14 in his History of Cornell says "the presidency of Deane Malott may come to be termed the Era of Well-Being."

"Never in our history have we had such a period of building. The expense has been met by State appropriations and by gifts in sums hitherto undreamed of. The budget increased by 120 per cent, to over a hundred million dollars. Research came to rival teaching as the business of the University.

"The administrative structure of the University has been profoundly altered, rationalized, and strengthened. To some, who regard all administration as a usurpation of faculty rights, this is a cause of grief; but it is hard to conceive how the far-flung and fantastically diverse affairs of the University can be handled with less administration.

"In the strictly educational business of the University the President has intervened little. We know, however, that he is deeply concerned about the improvement, the personalizing, of teaching. He deplores mass procedures and the lack of reward for the good or even brilliant teacher who is not fecund of learned articles. Some steps have been taken in this regard.

"The material state of the Faculty has markedly improved. Never since the 1890's has the Faculty been so well at ease. And the President has stoutly defended the rights of teachers to tenure, security, freedom of expression, freedom of conscience, freedom to teach.

"The state of the students has likewise been bettered. The deplorable absence of proper housing has been corrected or will be corrected. Responsible care is extended to student souls, minds, and bodies. The opportunities for religious development, for the preservation of health, for physical and social recreation, are such as have never before existed at Cornell."

James A. Perkins became the seventh President of Cornell July 1, 1963. Since 1951 he had been vice-president of the Carnegie Corporation and since 1955, vice-president of the Carnegie Foundation for the Advancement of Teaching.

Born October 11, 1911, in Philadelphia, Pa., President Perkins received the AB at Swarthmore in 1934; at Princeton the MA in 1936, PhD in 1937. He stayed at Princeton

President James A. Perkins

until 1941, first as instructor of political science, later as assistant professor and assistant director of the School of Public and International Affairs. During World War II he was in Washington in the Office of Price Administration and Foreign Economic Administration; returned to Swarthmore in 1945 for five years as vice-president.

On the day of his inauguration as President of Cornell, Perkins was appointed chairman of a newly created Regents advisory committee on educational leadership for the future, to investigate means of improving administration of higher education in New York State. He is a member of the general advisory committee of the U.S. Arms Control & Disarmament Agency of the U.S. Commission for UNESCO, and of a committee appointed by Governor Hughes of New Jersey to study higher education opportunities and needs in that state. He founded the Council of Higher Education in the American Republics; was a co-author of a Rockefeller Panel Report on "The Power of the Democratic Idea," and with his colleagues is continuing studies of democratic growth in developing countries. President Lyndon Johnson appointed him to a special advisory committee on U.S. foreign policy.

He was the first board chairman of the Foundation Library Center; is a trustee of Rand Corp., a non-profit corporation that advises the Air Force, of Memorial Sloan-Kettering Cancer Center of New York, and of the Council on Foreign Relations. He is a director of Carnegie Foundation for Advancement of Teaching, Educational Testing Service, and Teachers Insurance & Annuity Association. President Perkins is a member of the Society of Friends, as was Ezra Cornell.

New College of Engineering quadrangle between Campus Road and Cascadilla gorge. Clockwise from upper left: Phillips Hall, Electrical Engineering; Upson Hall, Mechanical Engineering, with Grumman Hall, Aerospace Engineering, far wing; Nuclear Reactor Laboratory (along gorge); Kim-ball, Thurston & Bard Halls (connected), Materials & Metallurgy; Hollister Hall, Civil Engineering; Carpenter Hall, administration & Library. Across Campus Road (*center*) is Olin Hall, Chemical Engineering. Near lower right, below Central Avenue, is the Gannett Medical Clinic.

Dr. Connie M. Guion MD '17, long-time teacher at the Medical College and physician at The New York Hospital, at a Medical Center addition named for her.

Cornell Glee Club is directed in Sage Chapel by Prof. Thomas A. Sokol, Music. During Christmas recess, 1960, the Club gave concerts in Moscow, Leningrad & London; and the Glee Club of 1963 after Commencement had a fifteen-day concert tour of England.

New libraries at heart of Campus. To make easily accessible the new John M. Olin Library and its adjoining Uris Library for undergraduates (center above), Tower Road was changed to turn on Sage Avenue, its lower end now a walk; and the course of Central Avenue now goes to the west of Uris Library, along the brow of Library slope.

Boardman Hall goes down. Wall of former Law School building topples as it is demolished preparing site for the John M. Olin Library.

New suspension bridge across Fall Creek was designed by Profs. S. C. Hollister and William McGuire MCE '47. Not so "springy" as the bridge on the same site that was found to be unsafe after sixty years, this is the fourth footbridge over this part of Fall Creek.

Main lobby and service desk of John M. Olin Library. Stone of wall at right rear is from Boardman Hall and one of the carved stone gargoyles saved from Boardman Hall can just be seen. The building is a model library.

Uris Library is the original University Library building thoroughly and attractively remodelled and furnished for books and services principally for undergraduates.

Noyes Lodge replaced the Johnny Parson Club as a place for meeting and eating on the coast of Beebe Lake. Footbridge crosses above Triphammer Falls. Walk at right leads to women's dormitories.

"How to Grow a Musical" troupe from Cornell Dramatic Club toured six Latin American countries with performances on stage, television, radio, and informally, under auspices of U.S. Department of State. Pictured (*from left*) are Pamela Trimby '65, Judith Halpern '63, Carol Androsky '64, Joan Lazarus '64, Maureen McGuire '62, Joanne Lewis '63, David Green '62, Janice Perlman '65, Linda Kopp '62, Brian Cooper '62, Jeffrey Kahn '63, Scott Gibbs '63.

Old Zeta Psi house near Stewart Avenue bridge, purchased by University from American Legion, is demolished for a parking lot.

Winter Heptagonal Games championship meets have turned away spectators from Barton Hall since 1946.

At University of Heidelberg, Germany, Cornellians dedicate a plaque to President Jacob Gould Schurman in New College (Schurman Hall), which was built with funds he got from Americans when he was U.S. Ambassador to Germany. At the ceremonies (*from left*): U.S. Ambassador Walter C. Dowling, Birge W. Kinne '16, Trustee Chairman Arthur H. Dean '19, Heidelberg Rektor Gottfried Koethe, President Deane W. Malott, Donald R. Baldwin '16, Heidelberg Registrar F. Hinz. Heidelberg and Cornell exchange Schurman Fellowship students.

Steven M. Machooka '64 of Kenya was called Cornell's best distance runner in fifty years. As a Sophomore he never lost a cross country race and was Intercollegiate (*above*) and Heptagonals champion. The next year he set new Cornell records for the mile: indoors 4 min. 13.6 sec.; outdoors 4:10.5.

Track team co-captain John S. Murray '61 set pole-vault records for the Heptagonal Games: indoors 14 ft. 5 in.; outdoors 14 ft. 7½ in.

Varsity football players carry their new coach, Tom Harp, off Franklin Field after their 31–0 victory over Penn in 1961, the first under his tutelage and the first Pennsylvania shutout since 1939. No. 18 is Co-capt. D. E. McKelvey '62; No. 64 G. F. Page '62; No. 57 A. P. Turel Jr. '63.

Undefeated by any college, the 1963 crew lost the final heat of the Henley Royal Regatta to University of London. *From left:* Stroke G. Bettle III '65, D. L. Krez '65, J. A. Rothschild '65, D. S. Light '64, J. H. Nunn '65, A. F. Thomasson '63, G. R. Hough '65, M. McGuirk '63. Coxwain J. M. Beeman '64.

Record-setting Quarterback Gary F. Wood '64 carries off-tackle in 1963 Homecoming thriller against Yale that Cornell won, 13–10. Running his interference is Guard (67) David L. Mellon '65. Wood broke five major all-time Cornell and Ivy League records in phases of offensive play.

Helen Newman Hall, women's sports building on the north shore of Beebe Lake, is the gift of Floyd R. Newman '12, and named for his wife. Women's dormitories in foreground are *(from left)* Mary Donlon, Clara Dickson, and Balch Halls. At upper left are the University-built Pleasant Grove Apartments for upperclass and married students, near University Observatory.

University Halls, six dormitories for men, form a quadrangle above Stewart Avenue and below the World War I Memorial towers. At right center Hughes Hall, new Law School residence, adjoins Myron Taylor Hall along Cascadilla Creek. Between Barton Hall and Tower Road (*center*), remodelled Veterinary College buildings and new Ives Hall house the School of Industrial & Labor Relations. In the distance, above upper Alumni Field and Kite Hill parking lot, at right is Riley-Robb Hall for Agricultural Engineering. Large building beyond on Tower Road is Morrison Hall for Animal Husbandry. At end of Tower Road, part of the new Veterinary College can be seen.

P. C. Mountan '66 drives polo ball toward Yale goal in the Riding Hall.

At his Fifty-year Reunion Emerson Hinchliff '14 chats with Prof. Harry Caplan '16, Classics. Hinchliff celebrated by giving the University $250,000 for a professorship in Spanish literature.

At Class Reunions Alumnae Secretary Pauline J. Schmid '25 greets seventy-year alumni Frederick W. Field '94 (left), Mrs. Clark & Thomas S. Clark '94.

NCAA wrestling champions of three eras. *From left:* Frank A. Bettucci '53, Glenn D. Stafford '30, Donald G. Dickason '53, David C. Auble '60.

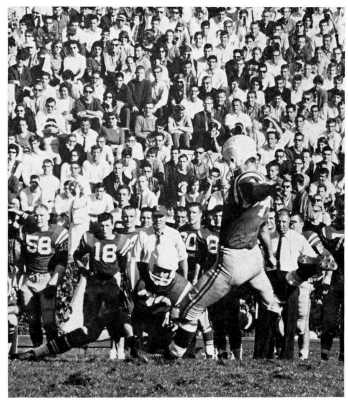

Peter K. Gogolak '64 kicks a 50-yard field goal against Lehigh, J. B. Docherty '66 holding. Gogolak set a national record for major colleges with 44 consecutive points kicked after touchdowns. He made good 54 of his 55 total conversion attempts and 9 of 27 total field-goal attempts as a Cornell player.

Intercollegiate polo champions 1963 (Cornell led in seven of nine years, except only 1957 & 1960). *From left:* Coach Prof. S. J. Roberts '38, Capt. J. R. Morse '63, P. Dix '63, P. C. Mountan '66, J. H. Suwinski '65, Asst. Coach F. H. Page.

Cornell's Ionospheric Observatory near Arecibo, Puerto Rico, has world's largest radar-radio telescope: a transmitter platform suspended high above a 19-acre receiving "dish." It was conceived and its operation for studying the earth's upper ionisphere is directed by Prof. William E. Gordon PhD '53 for the University's Center for Radiophysics & Space Research. Construction cost of nearly $9 million was met by the U.S. Department of Defense.

Prof. Hans A. Bethe received the 1961 Enrico Fermi Award of the U.S. Atomic Energy Commission: "For contributions to nuclear and theoretical physics, to peaceful uses of atomic energy, and to the security of the United States." A gold medal and $50,000 accompanied his citation. Dismissed from University of Tubingen, Germany, when Hitler came to power, Prof. Bethe joined the Cornell Faculty in 1935.

Peace Corps candidates training at University take their daily running stint through Andrew D. White Gate at top of Eddy Street.

Awaiting their calls to form the academic procession to the Centennial Convocation, delegates from 116 colleges and universities are seated on the Quadrangle in order of their institutions' founding. Delegate of earliest is at near right: University of Bologna, Italy, 1000 A.D.

Centennial celebration speakers Adlai E. Stevenson, U.S. Ambassador to the United Nations, and Sir Eric Ashby, Master of Clare College, Cambridge, with President James A. Perkins.

President James A. Perkins, University officers and Trustees review Centennial procession from terrace steps of John M. Olin Library, from there to join procession on its march from Quadrangle to Barton Hall.

New Physical Sciences Building rises to connect Baker Laboratory (*foreground*) and Rockefeller Hall. At upper center, beyond Bailey Hall, is Malott Hall for the Graduate School of Business & Public Administration; across Tower Road, buildings of the School of Industrial & Labor Relations. At left, below Bailey Hall, are Savage Hall for the Graduate School of Nutrition, Floyd R. Newman Laboratory for Nuclear Studies and its Synchrotron Building.

To start the University's second century, Vice Provost T. W. Mackesey (*right*) announced more than $82 million of construction underway and planned to start soon. He predicted that by 1980 Cornell's 12,000 students in Ithaca would increase to at least 17,500; graduate students more than doubling, from about 3000 to 7000; undergraduates increasing from 9000 to 10,500. Prof. Mackesey and President James A. Perkins show model of new $30 million Science Center around enlarged Baker Laboratory and renovated Rockefeller Hall.

"I am thinking tonight of my old college town,
I am dreaming of days that are flown."

INDEX